TABOO
OR TO DO?

TABOO OR TO DO?

Is Christianity complementary with yoga, martial arts, Hallowe'en, mindfulness and other alternative practices?

ROSS CLIFFORD & PHILIP JOHNSON

Foreword by John Drane

DARTON · LONGMAN + TODD

To Beverley and Ruth

First published in 2016 by Darton, Longman and Todd Ltd
1 Spencer Court
140–142 Wandsworth High Street
London SW18 4JJ

ISBN 978-0-232-53253-1

A catalogue record for this book is available from the British Library.

Designed and typeset by Judy Linard

Printed and bound in Great Britain by Bell & Bain, Glasgow

CONTENTS

CONTENTS

FOREWORD

Wherever you look, Western culture is in a state of flux, if not considerable upheaval. Ideas and attitudes that have been taken for granted for generations no longer seem to work, and nowhere is this more obvious than in the world of belief. There is a significant rise in the number of people who say they have no faith, yet religion is a more constant feature of the news headlines than has been the case for decades. As long ago as 1971, John Lennon's classic song 'Imagine' heralded a world with 'no religion', but the secular tsunami that many expected has never quite materialized – at least, not in the form that he envisaged. We seem to be in a contradictory shadowland in which we have become both less religious and more religious, depending on where you look and whose opinion you listen to. One thing is clear: secularism is no longer what it once was, and even those who claim to have no religion are unlikely to be atheists, while many non-religious individuals happily describe themselves as 'spiritual'.

Fifty years ago, spirituality and religion would have been assumed to be two sides of the same coin. But in today's search for meaning, wholeness, and purpose, people embrace a bewildering variety of practices and therapies – many of which are rooted in traditional world faiths but are being adapted in ways that distance them from their origins while still preserving the sort of mystical overtones that are common to all religious traditions. For many Christians, this eclectic mix is at best confusing and at worst might even be seriously damaging. Hence the title of this book: should practices which range from tarot cards to animal blessings be condemned as dangerous, or embraced as evidence of God at work in today's world?

TABOO OR TO DO?

After an overview of Christian approaches to such questions, Ross Clifford and Philip Johnson go on to examine a selection of such practices, in each case giving an account of their origins and history (and often challenging urban myths and Christian prejudices) before offering their own theological perspectives along with suggestions for positive engagement with practitioners and further questions for reflection and discussion. Their understandings are well grounded in an extensive ministry in mind, body, spirit festivals not only in their own native Australia but in other parts of the world as well. This was the context in which I first encountered them myself, now almost twenty years ago. My wife Olive and I were teaching an intensive course at the theological college in Sydney where Ross is principal, and in conversation about training for mission he mentioned taking groups of students to one of the world's biggest spiritual festivals in Darling Harbour, and their use of tarot cards in talking about Christian faith. I had a longstanding interest in esoteric spirituality going back to my own doctoral studies in Gnosticism (an ancient philosophy that in many ways was rebranded as the 'new age') and the notion that something apparently 'non-Christian' might actually lead people to Christ not only made theological sense to me, but was also clearly effective as more than one of the ordinands in the class that Olive and I were teaching had found Christian faith through that medium.

In this book Ross and Philip offer practical examples of Christian ministry with those who are searching for meaning through 'alternative' beliefs and practices; also they explain how this relates to the Bible and historic theological understandings. They connect with recent thinking on the *missio Dei* that effective missional engagement begins with identifying where God is already at work. This is a helpful corrective of alarmist attitudes. They guide us through issues where we may feel uncomfortable and address questions many are exploring in the quest for life-giving and empowering answers.

John Drane, Trinity Sunday 2016

STARTING THE
CONVERSATION ...

We were out walking our dogs through a nearby park where two Jehovah's Witnesses were seated with a small display rack of pamphlets. A few yards away were a couple of people practising T'ai Chi to taped music. All this is directly opposite a shopping centre where a gym advertises fitness exercises and the martial arts. Down the road is a church that is offering yoga. This is just one snapshot of the global village and it illustrates how close some 'taboo' or 'to do' activities are to our front doorsteps.

We are exploring in these chapters how in our multi-cultural neighbourhoods we as Christians and churches are encountering and responding to Eastern religious practices and traditions. There are other public practices such as Hallowe'en that we will also consider. There is a spirituality we are rubbing against in the public square.

Now, this is not a book about whether the western world is in post-Christendom. There is a top-heavy pile of books that sift through that question. There are plenty of surveys which substantiate the point with lots of statistics. In some places there is extraordinary questioning about the existence of Jesus as well as if he could be God.[1] Then in other places the issues are on other topics. In England it is reported that Church of England attendance rates have fallen dramatically to less than one million people each week.[2] We get overwhelmed by all that data and think it's so depressing we want to give up. Yet we want to make it clear at the start that the research is pretty clear that the West is not becoming less spiritual, but rather less and less Christian. There is plenty of room still for having conversations about Jesus and faith, and God does surprising things when we least expect it. And we don't want to paint too gloomy a picture because good things are taking place in the global Church.

Apart from anecdotal stories, we feel that we can sharpen our understanding from some of the latest evidence that points to spiritual inclinations in our neighbourhoods.

The Spirit of Things Unseen: belief in post-religious Britain is a wide-ranging report which has this telling comment in its executive summary:

> For all that formalised religious belief and institutionalised religious belonging has declined over recent decades, the British have not become a nation of atheists or materialists. On the contrary, a spiritual current runs as, if not more, powerfully through the nation than it once did.[3]

The report points out that over three-quarters of all adults (77%) and three-fifths (61%) of non-religious people believe that 'there are things in life that we simply cannot explain through science or any other means'. A majority of people still are believers in the existence of some kind of spiritual being, whether it is God or some universal life force.[4]

The USA reveals via the *2014 U.S. General Social Survey* some drift away from Christianity as these statistics indicate. For example 7.5 million Americans have abandoned organised religion since 2012 and 34% of Americans say they never attend worship services.[5] Perhaps a more worrying statistic from a Barna study is that nearly six in ten Millennials who grew up in churches leave and join the ranks of those who have no religious affiliation.[6]

However, the USA is also experiencing the 'spiritual but not religious' phenomena. A number of teachers in the USA like Deepak Chopra, Oprah Winfrey and Wayne Dyer are major spokespersons for the phenomena, and their influence reaches beyond America as they have exported their ideas around the world through books, magazines and syndicated TV shows. The latest vanguard expression is Oprah's new television series, *Belief*, which is 'dedicated to exploring the power of religion as a force for good across the globe'. [7] Elizabeth Gilbert expresses this so well:

'As people remake religion for themselves today, they are replacing adherence to fixed doctrine with the personal power of spiritual experience to transform their lives'.

Diana Butler Bass
https://www.washingtonpost.com/news/acts-of-faith/
wp/2015/10/18/oprahs-new-belief-series-shows-how-
dramatically-the-nature-of-faith-is-shifting/

Flexibility is just as essential for divinity as is discipline. Your job, then, should you choose to accept it, is to keep searching for the metaphors, rituals and teachers that will help you move ever closer to divinity ... As one line from the Upanishads suggests: 'People follow different paths, straight or crooked, according to their temperament, depending on which they consider best, or most appropriate – and all reach you, just as rivers enter the ocean. [8]

If you come to the southern hemisphere you will find that it is a similar story for Australia; it's a place for spiritual exploration but often outside the church.

Mark McCrindle is a social researcher who has taken the pulse of the Australian religious landscape. His findings (shown below) which resemble the trends in other countries, are that the two categories 'spiritual but not religious' and 'none' are each in their own right larger than all brands of Protestant combined.

Australians and religions[9]

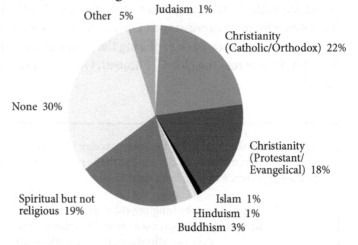

Other 5%   Judaism 1%

Christianity
(Catholic/Orthodox) 22%

None 30%

Christianity
(Protestant/
Evangelical) 18%

Spiritual but not
religious 19%

Islam 1%
Hinduism 1%
Buddhism 3%

On the world's stage the 'spiritual but not religious' and the 'none' are the two major categories. Elsewhere we have highlighted the two common characteristics of 'spiritual but not religious' as highly eclectic and a focused on self-spirituality. With respect to eclectic, it simply means there is a highly diverse range of sources and rituals. The transformative search occurs outside the Church and traditional religious services. It often incorporates a mix of things like a bit of Buddhist meditation, feng shui advice, Hindu ideas, and parts of Jesus' teaching.

The element of self-spirituality is focused on being the best person we can possibly be. This transformative journey leads to service of others, after one's own personal journey and discovery. Krista Tippett suggests that there is a real evolution in spiritual growth amongst such seekers since the 1980s and whilst not everyone is on a deep journey she feels they are more profound than dismissive stereotypes imply.[10]

A common mistake that is made is to directly associate the category of 'none' with the New Atheism. The 'none' group is much larger than irreligious atheists, and includes those who refuse to accept any label whilst being open to a spiritual dimension. Missional Church authority Ed Stetzer when commenting on a Pew Report on American Spirituality noted, 'those who don't identify with a faith are still remarkably spiritual ... more than 6 in 10 religiously unaffiliated Americans still believe in God and 1 in 5 say they pray daily. Yet such percentages are on the decline.'[11] They choose to be unaffiliated, do not live within a specific religious tradition, and dislike being pigeon-holed by the census labels that refer to traditional religions.

One helpful way of explaining the social phenomena of the 'nones' is to recall the global reaction to the death of the Australian cricketer Phil Hughes. His helmet did not protect him from a fast delivery of a cricket ball, which struck him in the back of the head and he died shortly afterwards in hospital. The social reaction worldwide from cricketers, coaches, and well-wishers beyond the game were uniformly saying 'our thoughts and prayers' are with Phil's family and he is watching from above. After a short hiatus in test matches, the Australian test cricket captain scored a century, and as a sign of honour he waved his bat to the heavens indicating that this innings was for Phil. This expression of hope was not connected to churches or an evangelist's revival but rather where Aussies and the rest of the West are at. A similar thing happened as a global response to the death of Diana, Princess of Wales and the city-wide terrorist attacks in Paris and Brussels.

Today we see many people who gravitate to 'spiritual but not religious' or 'none' juggling lots of balls. The balls being juggled often consist of spiritual tools scooped up from all kinds of East Asian religious practices and traditions. One of the points arising from *The Spirit of Things Unseen* report is that many people from both the religious and non-religious categories have had personal experiences of various spiritual practices. This Theos report indicates that 39% of the overall population admits to trying out certain things like tarot, astrology, reflexology, aura-readings; this includes 38% of the non-religious, compared to 40% of the religious. The list in the report is far from exhaustive, and probably the results would be higher if more prominent tools like Reiki had been included in the survey. We should note the fact that women are more likely to experiment with these things as compared to men.[12]

Many of the same balls are also being juggled by Christians. Churches are dabbling with all kinds of spiritual practices. Some do so as part of missional outreach activities, others take things up for personal growth. Some churches hire out their halls where classes are taught in these practices. At the personal level, many are doing yoga at the gym and combining alternative therapies as part of a way of life. Some encourage their children to take lessons in martial arts. You could say that the kit-bag is bulging with the gear we need to flourish, and most of us want to feel right about the way we are navigating through the puzzles and passages of life. The perennial challenge seems to be, do we condemn or participate?

The honest question is this, are we ready to have a conversation about all these balls - that is the practices that we have selected as chapter topics such as yoga, and T'ai Chi?

WHAT DOES THIS CONVERSATION LOOK LIKE?

It's helpful to pause and take a look at how some Christians have responded to these issues. You may decide at the moment that you want to take the plunge by reading one of the chapters that takes your interest. You may find after jumping into a chapter that you will want to take a look at what we are about to say here.

One way to get a grip of the background issues to each topic is to tease out the chief characteristics and style that turns up in Christian books. One of us devised an interpretative grid that identified different kinds of approaches and it has turned out to be a tool that is adaptable.[13] The grid refers to particular styles and highlights the strengths and limitations of each one. The styles have these labels:

We have been involved in public debates on Sunday afternoons where the big question is, 'Is Jesus God in human flesh?' We have responded to challenges where some religious groups, like the Christadelphians, deny the Bible teaching that Jesus is divine. This is the *heresy* approach. What we do in this approach is to assess a tool or practice such as yoga from the standpoint of the main doctrines of the Christian worldview. A tool or practice will be tested for its conformity or deviation from doctrines such as the Trinity, Christ's deity, atonement and resurrection. If the practice or belief is linked to another religion, or has the strong potential to lead into accepting another faith, then it will be rejected. One strength in this approach is that it encourages us to be discerning and to know why we believe what we believe. There are foundations to stand on which can inform a critical conversation on a given issue. However, it has a tendency to be rigid and inflexible. Not all these matters are reducible to the binary black/white choice. Quite a few practices are rooted in universal insights like using or moving your body. In the heresy approach there tends to be more emphasis on contrasting views without there being much room for genuinely listening to the other person. Not everyone is necessarily interested in making contrasts and comparisons, and it is possible that we can rebuff a person without having ever heard their story or the narrative.[14]

The *spiritual warfare* approach has a strong emphasis on resisting spiritual deception with a focus on prayer in our discipleship. If a belief or practice is rooted in a non-Christian religion the concern may be expressed that it is spiritually tainted and perhaps under a demonic curse. In some expressions of this movement, anyone who has been exposed to, or been a practitioner of, a suspect practice is regarded as being under the influence or control of satanic powers. The remedy is to release the person from these bondages through prayer and/or an exorcistic ritual. Perhaps the great strength of this approach is that it takes seriously the problem of spiritual deception being linked to harmful spirits. We explore this point in the chapter on angels. However, a serious weakness in this approach is that it can get out of hand. Christians risk ending up in an unbiblical, almost superstitious, kind of dualism. Too much attention can be given to the Devil rather than affirming the sovereignty and power of God in all realms. It may make Christians feel too defensive and closed-off from listening to sincere non-Christian people who may not have any real religious worldview. Our pastoral concern for people may be off-putting to a seeker who feels they are being demonised and not taken seriously.

Such matters are not easily reduced to being just black or white. One of us spoke about alternative spiritualities in a church that is situated in a mountain-region where these alternatives are very popular. A few months afterwards a man who was strongly committed as a practitioner to many alternative therapies visited that church and made a faith commitment. He quickly realised that he had to sort out what he was going to do with his life, particularly since his entire livelihood rested on being a practitioner. He was referred on by the church to have a chat with us about his quandary. He could appreciate that many of the practices were compatible with being a follower of Jesus but others were spiritually compromising. As he tried to reach a resolution he found that the local church was not quite able to help him through the dilemma. The church had the 'truth' but seemed to lack 'spiritual power' and discernment. He joined a charismatic church where they appreciated the problem of spiritual discernment and warfare. He did not feel that it was legitimate to dump the baby with the bath water nor did he feel at ease continuing as a practitioner. In the end he found that for his own spiritual growth and sanity that he had to walk away from his practice. His journey highlights the tension points of 'taboo or to do', as well as underscoring that it is far too simplistic to reduce everything down to binary categories. Life is not that straight-forward and in the process of careful discernment we can discover that not all practices are inherently demonic or tainted.

Like the above case, the *testimony* model is very much about the personal story of those who have been practitioners and have then found faith in Christ. The testimony of an ex-practitioner has good lessons we can benefit from. A person who has been an 'insider' has a perspective on things that can be valuable. The great strength of the testimony model is that it is grounded in real life experiences, and it allows a person to share how they have come to faith. There is, however, an ever-present limitation that we must be mindful about. While a testimony can serve as a warning that some practices are problematic or possibly dangerous, the story should not always be taken at face-value. It is good to ask discerning questions about whether the story is fair and honest and not the result of bitter distortion. Sometimes we need to ask about a person's bona fides because this is an area where many high profile reputations have been built on 'fake' testimonies. If it is not a fair testimony that allows for a mutual time of sharing then it may break down into bickering, shouting and name-calling. We must keep in mind that a testimony works both ways because there are plenty of ex-Christians who can tell stories of being disappointed. A generation has been impacted by Elizabeth Gilbert's testimony of the eclectic search in *Eat, Pray, Love.*

The next approach is the *end-times conspiracy*. This approach tends to evaluate non-Christian practices in a grid to detect things that are signs of the Antichrist and of churches becoming apostate. These are understood to be signs that Christ's Second Advent is imminent. Practices like yoga are identified with the spirit of Antichrist; and the tendency among some Christians to embrace yoga is interpreted as a sign of apostasy within the church. A characteristic of this approach is to filter information through a paradigm of conspiracy: behind the scenes some people are planning to create a global crisis that will pave the way for the Antichrist to appear. The strength of this approach is that it reinforces the need for Christians to be discerning and watchful. However, its great drawback is that it is highly speculative in interpreting events and practices as signs of the end, it fosters a high level of judgmental reactions, and life is much more messy and complicated than conspiracy theories allow for in understanding matters.

Some years ago Francis Schaeffer set up in Switzerland a Christian village called L'Abri ('The Shelter'). It continues today, and his followers are scattered all around the world. He developed the *cultural* approach to apologetics where art, music, philosophy, law, and history were looked at through the eyes of Christian faith. Schaeffer found he could help people to reflect more on their own views of life via these aspects of culture. For example, he loved to take people to an art gallery and to sit and ponder the meaning of paintings and sculptures. He encouraged people to look at some of the classic paintings from Christian artists like Rembrandt, and to compare that with for example the paintings of Picasso.

The essence of this approach is to see all spheres of life make the best sense when viewed through the lens of Christian faith. What goes hand-in-glove with this approach is identifying what aspects of culture are undergirded by a religious worldview. The great strength of this approach is looking at life on a large canvas. This approach can be very amenable to in-depth conversations on ultimate meaning of all aspects of life but it does have some limitations. One drawback is that it can go in a philosophical direction that does not suit people who are unaccustomed to logical big-picture thinking. For people who don't have any affinity with Christianity this approach seems irrelevant or even arrogant. Most people today get irritated when someone tells them their understanding of life is illogical and contradictory. They can legitimately say, 'Why should I start with your worldview I've got my own'.

The *incarnational* approach takes a different tack from the others in that it is prepared to venture into the marketplace and is not restricted to a purely defensive stance. There is a strong emphasis on participating in dialogue and conversations in all kinds of contexts. It can, and often does, partake of some of the good features of the other approaches with respect to having critical discernment. However, it is not limited to mere analysis that evaluates practices solely to find weaknesses and faults. It encourages an understanding of other worldviews but is also centred in finding positive points of contact. Like Paul in Athens, (Acts 17:16-34), who entered the Athenian marketplace and chatted to anyone as well as the philosophers in the Areopagus Council, there is a willingness to find elements that can be framed in a Christian understanding. Paul gave a Christian perspective to quotes he found among Stoic philosophers - 'in him we live and move and have our being' and 'we are his offspring'. He opened up a conversation where he could not merely detect weaknesses but also found positive evidence of God being at work. The incarnational approach involves stepping out of comfort zones and being vulnerable to experiencing the points of tension that arise when we encounter practices. It goads us into critical reflections rather than formulaic black/white answers. A good incarnational conversation will look for positive points to build a constructive way forward that does not compromise nor insist on demonising everything that seems 'alien'. This approach is receiving wide acclaim in missional circles.[15]

Our personal interactions with the kinds of practices in this book are built around an incarnational approach. In the 1990s we co-founded The Community of Hope exhibitor's booth in Mind*Body*Spirit festivals, and similar kinds of spiritual exhibitions are found around the world. For churches to enter into these festivals is not difficult. We rang the festival organisers to see if we could have a prayer-chair, and there was some initial hesitation because we are Christian. After a brief reflection the organisers contacted us and were happy to allow us in as long as we did not demonise others. We soon found ourselves being contacted by churches and para-church ministries, which further opened up other avenues to be involved among non-Christian festivals. We were able to operate as followers of Jesus by taking part at festivals in a spirit of dignity and respect, and we found ourselves working through many questions that relate to alternate practices like tarot, mind powers, astrology, and meditation.[16] Some of the activities that we developed there for facilitating good conversations are subjects that we will touch on in different parts of this book.

Why Christmas and Easter?

As we seek to make connections with people via various spiritual practices, we can be criticised for the approach we take. One response we often make is, think about Christmas and Easter. These have both been 'tainted' with Pagan connections that the Church decided to take over and reframe with a whole new meaning. The Christian dating of Christmas is around 350 AD and it appears that it absorbed a couple of Pagan European festivals including a feast in honour of Saturn. It was surrounded by merriment associated with the winter solstice. The church leaders had to repeatedly remind people that the focus was on worshipping Christ the true Son and not the older pagan emphasis on Saturn and the Sun.

The origins of Easter are just as blurred. There was a decision made at the Council of Nicea (325 AD) to agree on observing Easter on the first full moon after the spring equinox which is a time of new birth. The date did not settle across the western church until the 800s, while the Eastern Orthodox churches followed a different calendar. Relying on Bede's *Ecclesiastical History* (731 AD) it has been claimed that Easter is a substitution for the worship of the goddess Eostre. This evidence is shadowy at best and the word Easter in an English context may derive from the Anglo-Saxon term Estor-monath which meant the month of new beginnings.[17] However, many symbols like Easter eggs have existed in Pagan cultures. Understandably, the eggs were taken as a symbol of the new life in Christ and often there was an absence of same during Lent. The household of Edward I distributed 450 eggs during a 1290 AD Easter celebration. The Easter Bunny has always been a Pagan symbol of fertility. The

Church ascribed a new meaning by placing a white rabbit in the hands of either Mary or the Christ child to symbolise the triumph of chastity over lust.

When we draw attention to the way the Church has wrestled with the transformation of these special days, there is generally an acknowledgement that this is a very good point. For many this is an 'Aha' moment.

We are all prone to being inconsistent or even hypocritical on some points. We are shaped by things that are part of our culture, and what's familiar we tend to take for granted, while anything that is not part of our cultural background we tend to be a bit suspicious about from the outset.

TABOO OR TO DO?

In this book we want to honestly start a conversation about these matters. We want to do so by opening up each chapter on a given practice like yoga, to sort out the relevant historical background and matters of origins. We want to tease out the issues for critical spiritual discernment, and to further illustrate matters by describing some case studies that involve different responses. *We note that sometimes as Christians we prohibit things, sometimes we Christianise, and sometimes we embrace things wholeheartedly.* Is it 'taboo or to do?' We do not believe there are any easy answers, and we do not pretend to claim that we have all the answers either. What we warmly offer you is the chance to join us in a journey of exploration and to converse with us and others in a spirit of gentleness and respect (1 Pet. 3:15).

1
YOGA –
One step too far?

Yoga is a spiritual discipline that is so popular that it saturates much of western life. It's a practice that is easily adopted and hardly anyone raises an eyebrow about it. We were driving up the main street of a town in Australia and noticed a mainline denominational church advertising yoga classes twice a week; while in England we've spotted a well-known charity unapologetically renting its facilities out for yoga classes.

Ross was visiting as a professor and practitioner at an American seminary. A number of faculty expressed concerns regarding the appropriateness of our Christian witness, and some of the connections we make, in spiritual festivals. Imagine his surprise when a faculty email was distributed asking for support for a yoga session where the instructor was a practitioner of Iyengar Yoga, which has a clear and strong root in the Hindu faith. We then discovered that in the Christian university, of which the seminary was part, all of the sports teams participated in this yoga class as part of their training.

Most of us could repeat anecdotes like this based on personal experiences, particularly as yoga is fairly common in work places, the gym, and in other places where people gather to do physical exercise and play sport. Yoga has become such a part of life that when one of us wrote a brief article about it in a church magazine, there was a backlash from some conservative churches who protested that they were doing yoga and had no problem with it. Yoga is so omnipresent that the question facing Christians about 'taboo or to do' is impossible to avoid. Diverse voices are being heard on the matter.

People understandably find yoga appealing because it involves a form of exercise and produces good feelings of relaxation. Many insist that they practice yoga just for the benefits of well-being and fitness, and have no interest in the spirituality that formed the basis of it.

A Google-based search lists thousands of websites from all western nations where Christians and local churches hold to a spectrum of views on yoga.

BACKGROUND

As pointed out in the introduction, this is a time when people are grasping spiritual practices and reframing them. Christians are among the throng of those who dabble and reframe materials. Some people also take elements out of Christianity, disconnect them from their source, and apply them in different ways to their lives. Of course we should ask the question, 'Is there a goal to yoga? Is it possible to reframe this discipline and remain consistent with our commitment to Christ?'

The word 'yoga' comes from a Sanskrit word and means 'to bind,' 'to yoke' or 'be in union with'. In classical Hindu terms Shiva is the god of yoga, although some may also refer to Brahman. Yoga is usually described by practitioners in the Indian subcontinent as a way of life, a philosophy, and a form of meditation. It is construed as a deeply inward journey where the distractions of both the exterior world and the rational mind are set aside. The goal of yoga is to achieve enlightenment and union with Shiva.

The earliest traces we have for the origins of yoga take us back to around 3000 BC in the Indus valley with a figurine seated in the lotus position. Yoga is spoken of in various Hindu sacred texts such as the Rig-Veda (5.81.1), and in the Katha Upanishad (2.6.10-11). The classic philosophical writing that sums it all up is in the Yoga Sutras of Patañjali.

TABOO OR TO DO?

There are many versions of yoga found in the Hindu traditions. The best known is called Hatha Yoga and this is the discipline where one learns and aspires to master all the bodily postures. It is this version of yoga that is most familiar in the west. However, it is important to note that a strict or proper understanding of Hatha Yoga involves much more than just physical fitness. The bodily postures have a specific goal which is about bringing your body under control so as to prepare your mind for the next step which is meditation. The traditional approach to meditation is definitely directed to a spiritual goal where one meditates on becoming enlightened about escaping from the cycle of life, death, and rebirth.

Another version known as Raja Yoga – royal yoga – has had different connotations in history depending on who is using the term. It may involve the guidance of a guru (teacher). The practice obviously includes the bodily postures but concentrates much more on attaining deep meditative states.

The Eight Limbs of Yoga

- Yama – restraint
- Niyama – observance
- Asana – physical posture
- Pranayama – breath control
- Pratyahara – withdrawal
- Dharana – concentration
- Dhyana – meditation
- Samadhi – self-collectedness

For some practitioners of Raja Yoga, the way to reach this deep meditation is facilitated by the use of a mantra that is chanted. The mantra consists of Sanskrit words that are repeated over and over. Another technique for meditation is using a mandala which is a picture of spiritual symbols that one meditates on. However, adherents of the Brahma Kumaris movement do not rely on mandalas and mantras.

In some traditional approaches there may be an act of devotion to the guru who is the physical embodiment of the sacred. One directs devotion toward the spark of divinity that is present in the guru, but with the understanding that the ultimate source is a deity (Shiva).

24

Bhakti Yoga is a devotional path where one accepts instruction from a guru whose teaching involves following a very rigorous way of life. A devotee will use the bodily postures in combination with specific meditative exercises, which may include chanting a hymn or mantra, as well as contemplating specific sacred texts. A well-known example of a Bhakti Yoga group is the Hare Krishna. Their founding teacher Acharya Bhaktivedanta Prabhupada taught the way of life through devotion to Lord Krishna. One relates to Lord Krishna through chanting the devotional mantra, and by meditating on the precepts found in the text the Bhagavad-Gita.

Another type of yoga which has attracted many celebrities is known as Siddha Yoga. This type of yoga became known outside India in the early 1970s when Swami Muktananda Paramahansa (1908-1982) toured America and Australia. Muktananda became known in many places as the 'guru's guru' because of his palpable presence and his ability to awaken people to deep spiritual experiences. Siddha Yoga is the unnamed tradition that Elizabeth Gilbert was delving into in India in her bestselling book *Eat, Pray, Love.*

What distinguishes Siddha Yoga is its emphasis on using various 'siddhis' or powers that may be awakened in meditative exercises. The exercises, which include some Hatha Yoga postures, are anchored in an understanding that our bodies contain seven major energy centres known as chakras. By chanting a long hymn known as the Guru-Gita, one may enter into an altered state of consciousness where each chakra is energised and one begins to have visions of ultimate reality (see the diagram below). The process where the chakras are 'opened' or energised is known as awakening the Kundalini. The Kundalini is symbolised as the uncoiling of a snake, which rises up through each chakra until it reaches the crown or third eye and one is released into the spiritual realm of Brahma. During Muktananda's life devotees were known to experience remarkable spontaneous bodily movements (kriyas), rhythmic breathing, dancing, crying, laughter, animal-like noises, and utterances in other tongues.

The Seven Chakras[1]

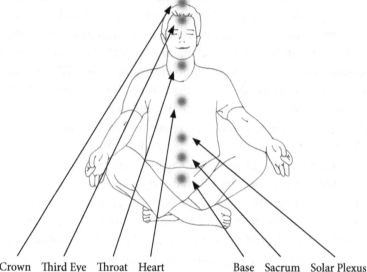

Crown   Third Eye   Throat   Heart   Base   Sacrum   Solar Plexus

It is worth noting that various aspects of yoga and its meditative traditions were carried over into the teachings of Gautama Buddha. The Buddhist way of life represented in part a break-away from the parent faith of Hindu beliefs.

Some of the traditional Hindu and Buddhist schools of yoga are taught in the West. However, as far as most westerners are concerned, yoga can be - and has been - uprooted from the strict confines of the Hindu and Buddhist traditions. Like many other things found beyond the western culture, yoga has been reshaped to suit the attitudes and lifestyle of the west. A good example of this attitude is found in Elizabeth Gilbert's words:

> True Yoga neither competes with nor precludes any other religion. You may use your Yoga - your disciplined practices of sacred union - to get closer to Krishna, Jesus, Mohammed, Buddha or Yahweh.[2]

CONTACT POINTS

For most of us, classes that offer the physical exercises of Hatha Yoga will be the likely entry point. The bodily postures have such popular appeal that they hardly need describing. Understandably, the bodily exercises are very appealing because many people look for a holistic way of living that improves health and well-being, and may produce a beneficial sense of serenity. That may be all there is. However, our exposure to yoga in this form may also open us up to a few key ideas that go hand-in-hand with the exercises, such as some breathing techniques, the concept of the chakras, and reincarnation.

In classic yoga teaching the goal of life is to break out of the cycle of life, death and rebirth that takes place on earth. It is a fundamental Hindu belief that at death one's soul may have to be reborn due to the deeds we have done in the present life. There is a universal law called karma which refers to the moral dimension of our lives. If we perform good deeds we accumulate 'good karma', and if we perform evil deeds we accumulate 'bad karma'. What we are reborn as in the next incarnation – an insect, reptile, fish, bird, mammal or human – will be determined by 'weighing' on a set of scales our good and bad karma. The worse your karma, the lower the form of life you return to, and the better your karma the higher up you will be. Yoga is a discipline that is meant to enable us to produce good karma, and, if we make a sufficiently good job of it, then we won't need to return to life on earth but will end up in union with Shiva.

It is sometimes the case that those who are already open to exploring the meaning of life through the prism of reincarnation find it is easy to gravitate to yoga. Much like the joining together of a horse and carriage, so the physical exercise of yoga attracts those who are open to believing in past lives.

For others the point of exposure may come via the chakras. The chakras are related to different parts of the body, such as the heart, throat and crown. One of us received a gift of a massage at a well-being centre. The masseur's technique included placing various stones over the body. Each stone was placed on those parts of the body where the chakras are located. Although the masseur was not personally committed to any belief in chakras this became part of the procedure.

DISCERNMENT

It appears that many Christians participate in yoga without asking any questions of discernment. Before we sift through some of the specific points that we should be concerned with, there is a basic truth that should be faced. It is relatively easy to become an armchair critic and to find faults with the various spiritual disciplines that are being explored in this book. However, it does not advance a conversation to present an argument for rejecting a particular technique or discipline. If you decide that yoga is taboo, then consider taking another step that supports a holistic and physical way of living.

In light of the models mentioned in the introduction, it is apparent that some Christians have raised critical concerns about using yoga. If you are operating from either a heresy or spiritual warfare viewpoint, then it is more likely that you will see yoga as being incompatible with Christian belief and practice. This may also be true for those who have strong affinities with the testimony model.

During the late twentieth century several commentators developed critical responses to yoga that were a product of the times. In the period from the 1960s to the 1980s yoga was primarily associated with various Hindu swamis or gurus. Many critical concerns swirled around the teaching and authority of the gurus, especially where such teaching diverged from classic Christian belief. Some of the big Indian gurus included Bhaktivedanta, and Muktananda, and TV show presenters such as Richard Hittleman (1927-1991). Nowadays, while guru groups still exist, the practice of yoga has broken out of those narrow boundaries and it is now mainstream.

Be Discerning of Different Forms of Hindu Yoga
• Iyengar yoga
• Satyananda yoga
• Tantra yoga
• Siddha yoga
• Raja yoga
• Bhakti yoga

A fair Christian critic of that era was John Allan who stated that 'the yoga systems of the East command respect ... they represent some of the greatest efforts of the human spirit'.[3] Among his concerns about some of the more 'magical' forms of yoga was the possibility in certain contexts of ending up in occult experiences. With respect to the more popular form of Hatha Yoga, he was not convinced that there was clear cut evidence to sustain alarms about occult influences.[4]

The three *substantial concerns* that were raised by various Christian apologists, and still are today, were:

(a) The uncritical acceptance of yoga on the basis that 'It works it must be fine' – experience taking priority over the place of scriptural authority and reasoned reflection about teachings and practice.

(b) With which deity is one being brought into union?

Often repeated biblical texts include: 'You shall have no other gods before me' (Ex. 20:3); 'Beware of false prophets' (Matt. 7:15); 'Beloved do not believe every spirit but test the spirits to see whether they are from God' (1 John 4:1).

(c) The other strand of criticism from that period is expressed by former yoga teachers who have become Christians. A very strong example of this is the testimony of Elizabeth Shier who taught yoga in South Africa. She indicated that practicing yoga had taken her into a spiritual place that was very empty and dark. She found it impossible to reconcile the practice of yoga, its meditative and bodily exercises, and its teachings with Christian faith. Her rejection of yoga allowed for no compromises.[5]

We have encountered people who have recently withdrawn from their prior commitments to New Spiritualities and who had included yoga in their way of life. We have found that for several individuals it is much too awkward for them to continue on with yoga, as it is too close to their pre-Christian way of life as healers or users of alternate spiritual tools. Some hold reservations about other Christians being interested in practising it.

However, as the experience of the global village has accelerated in very recent times, there are Christians who are conversant with the critical issues mentioned above but go on to insist that we need a much broader and deeper understanding. This is particularly apparent among those who grapple with questions about yoga in the context of missions. It is also the case among those who believe that some of the earlier models of response have weaknesses and limitations. They are not averse to a critically-informed use of yoga for well-being, fitness and personal enhancement. In these cases there are generally no grave worries about the physical postures and exercise. Rather, the concerns lie around the spiritual directions and techniques, such as using mantra meditation. One may regard exercises as being spiritual without necessarily being Hindu or Buddhist. If the facilitator is inviting you to adore a deity, then this is where the clear line of demarcation is drawn.

Christine Frost, who was born a Hindu but now is in the Orthodox Church, expresses it this way:

> Having sounded these warnings, I still believe that a modest yoga regimen can help us to stay supple in body and mind, spiritually alert and vigilant and ultimately live a Christian life with greater zest and joy. We can take our cue from the early church fathers. The Cappodocean Fathers were trained in pagan schools of rhetoric and logic but discarded the pagan ethos and deployed the techniques of their learning to brilliant effect in their Christian spiritual theology. Similarly, we too can deal with yoga without being swamped or led

astray by its alien ethos, provided we entrust ourselves to Christ our Lord, and our God.[6]

A pertinent point to keep in mind for the variety of the above positions is whether one is being drawn into worship of another god or not. When you read Continuing the Conversation you will realise that the following three issues have kept turning up throughout each chapter. First, the question concerns the role of the practitioner and the practice. For example it is possible to be involved in a discipline where the practitioner is explicitly neutral, whereas others will be advocates like the example mentioned earlier of the Christian university using Iyengar Yoga. Is it okay for the church to rent the hall to the first practitioner but not the second?

The second issue is what an individual may do as against a group. In an extensive report the Sydney Anglican Diocese sought to address this issue from their worldview perspective. It was noted that as yoga is often practiced in modern Sydney 'it is not necessarily problematic for believers'. For those who fear that such engagement with yoga might lead a less mature sister or brother astray (1 Cor. 8:9-12), they caution against having an 'overly tender conscience in this area' whilst 'being blind to our complicity in businesses, activities and communities in which human sinfulness is perpetuated'. However, it recommended that churches not rent out their premises to yoga classes on account of the spiritual confusion this may cause and they gave similar advice to its extensive school network. The report did urge 'clergy and laity alike to consider the missional significance of the wide uptake of yoga in recent decades'.[7]

The third issue is, is the origin of a discipline sufficient alone to rule something out? We discuss this question in more detail in the chapter on martial arts, including whether a religious practice has so evolved that it no longer has any real links with its origins. For example, the universal church celebrates Christmas and Easter even though they are 'tainted' with 'Pagan' origins and traditions. Also, we may be inconsistent in what we rule out;

that is we might dump yoga because of its Hindu origins but fail to rule out something else. In this context John Drane raises the helpful question as to whether there are any 'no-go' zones for God. In response to the book *Beyond Prediction: The Tarot and Your Spirituality*, which we co-wrote with John for the marketplace, he challenged critics:

> The one key theological question which we had to deal with in relation to the Tarot was this: does the *missio Dei* have limits? Can God be found at work, at least potentially, absolutely everywhere? Or is God's activity limited in some way? Put simply, are there 'no-go' areas for God? And if there are, what does this imply about our view of who God is? In the light of the consistent practice of both Jesus and Paul – not to mention my underlying conviction about who I think God really is – it would be theological and spiritual suicide to embrace an understanding that would exclude God from any area of human life, no matter how alien it might seem, or how threatening to conventional wisdom.[8]

CASE STUDIES

A Google search of yoga sites reveals many examples of churches who list yoga classes but the actual church website never advertises it. This seems to signify that these churches are simply operating in the general community and have no qualms about an open door to yoga classes. As we have seen other churches have taken public stands against permitting their facilities being used for yoga, and have spoken against Christians participating in such classes.

It is a point for discernment that some Hindus are not happy with Hatha yoga being commercialised and taken out of its original context. These critics also tend to find the Christian versions of yoga culturally and spiritually offensive. Religious studies scholar Andrea Jain has drawn attention to two polarised standpoints. One is the Christian 'yogaphobic' response which rejects everything on the basis that any sort of yoga is Hindu. The other response is from Hindus who protest at both the commercial reduction of Hatha Yoga, and at those who they believe are devaluing the Hindu essence of yoga.[9] A critical line of thinking then is if one chooses to practice 'Christian Yoga' will this create a stumbling block in meaningful outreach?

Also in this regard, how many westerners respond favourably to the trend of divorcing yoga from its spiritual context? Keep in mind then the outlook expressed by the best-selling author Elizabeth Gilbert who, in her own eclectic way, feels that it is vital to see yoga as something that is spiritually interconnected. She gives it this eclectic spiritual flavour:

> The Yogis believe a human life is a very special opportunity, because only in a human form and only with a human mind can God-realization ever occur. The turnips, the bedbugs, the coral – they never get a chance to find out who they really are. But we do have that chance. 'Our whole business therefore in this life,' wrote Saint Augustine, rather Yogically, 'is to restore to health the eye of the heart whereby God may be seen.' [10]

PraiseMoves

PraiseMoves, which began in the USA, has now found a home in England, Australia, and many other countries and local churches advertise it as a yoga alternative. Classes may be run during the week, and it is conceivable that it could be creatively adapted in particular church services. The creator of PraiseMoves, Laurette Willis, was once a practitioner of yoga and an adept of New Age, and she is utterly opposed to it. However, she offers a clear alternative that links prayer, praise and bodily postures so that one is centred in Christ. The distinguishing point here is that while traditional yoga is completely rejected, Laurette Willis is sensitive to the positive need to be holistic about the body, mind, emotions and spirit.[11] The exercises for the body are akin to yoga or aerobic exercises but practitioners are not just moving their limbs. Each set of exercises is accompanied by praise music or focuses on a scriptural passage so that your body, emotions, mind and spirit are drawn together.

CaraMayan is similar to PraiseMoves as it seeks to integrate dance and Christian spirituality as an alternative to yoga and T'ai Chi. It is strong on bodily postures and Pilates.[12]

Some of the familiar yoga postures for tummy, hips, thighs, and back include:

- Lotus position – seated cross-legged
- Chest breathing – elbows bent fingertips touching as you inhale
- Four Way Stretch – standing legs apart breathing, stretching forward arms parallel to floor, stretching backward, and stretching to the right and left
- Walking on all fours
- The Stork is lifting your left leg up to your groin
- Dancing posture – standing on your right foot and grasping from behind your left foot
- Salute to the Sun – often the final posture. Standing upright hands in prayer position, inhaling arms raised above your head, exhaling and bending forward until hands touch the floor, squatting on right leg left leg straight back, then right leg straight back hands on floor inhaling, then exhaling placing your forehead chest and knees on the floor, inhaling your thighs on the floor head and shoulders back, exhaling while making an arch of the body, holding breath left foot between hands and dropping to right knee, holding breath bringing right leg between hands and straightening knees, inhaling stretching hands above head, finally, exhaling, hands in prayer position and relaxing. [Some may be aware that there is a Christian alternative 'Salute to the Son', which involves similar postures but with the movements directed as a salute to the Trinity.]

Elsewhere we have spoken of biblically-based prayer postures:

- Kneeling as a sign of homage, emptiness and earnestness
- Hand movements, such as raised hands, spread-eagled hands,

palms turned upwards are signs of worship and opening ourselves to divine blessing
- Eyes raised and open as a sign that we are focused on the celestial realm and the strength and power therein
- Body work as a sign of our emotional status through drama, such as beating our breast.

Passages that help us on prayer postures are Ephesians 3:14, Philippians 2:10, Luke 5:8, Luke 22:41-42, Acts 7:60, Acts 9:40, 1 Timothy 2:8, Psalm 28:2, John 17:1, Daniel 6:10 and Luke 18:11-13.[13]

Bede Griffiths

Perhaps one of the more 'out there' ways for a Christian being immersed in another culture is the contemplative and dialogical way taken by Dom Bede Griffiths (1906-1993). As we will explore below, his entire discipline of yogic meditation takes one into a very deep path in places like India. Those who love the challenge of interacting in their faith in non-western settings, or developing ministries among ethnic communities, might be 'stretched' in every sense of the word by exploring Bede Griffiths' writings and meditative discipline.

He studied at Oxford under C. S. Lewis and then joined the Benedictines. His pilgrimage in faith led him to southern India where he established an ashram. For Griffiths the practice of yogic meditation incorporated the familiar Hatha yoga postures, as well as the cultural mode for both silent and audible meditation. In his approach one could incorporate words from scripture, and Christian prayers, alongside excerpts of phrases taken from Indian texts like the Bhagavad-Gita. This echoes in some respects Paul's willingness to quote the Stoic poets in Acts 17 'in him we live and move and have our being'. Paul gave these Stoic words a Christian sense as he dialogued with the philosophers in Athens.

Griffiths' way involved a Christian-based approach to yoga that was contextually sensitive to the Indian culture. It had the elements of being highly meditative and contemplative, with a focus on spiritual discipline and growth centred in the Trinity. At the same time it was also a practice that allowed for a meeting of minds and adepts outside of Christianity. Christians and traditional Hindus might meditate side by side. He believed that there was great integrity and value for Christians to reappropriate the mystical experience of faith, and that this could be reignited through his approach to yogic meditation. He also saw his discipline as opening up a dialogue with Hindus. He used specific Christian words or phrases as mantras like repeating the word 'Maranatha' (Lord Come) or 'Serve the living Christ'.

Holy yoga

Our colleague, and author on shaping the future church, Mike Frost, recounted an experience that is probably common to many of us. He was speaking at a conference on the US west coast and a leader approached him and said that he loved Mike's books. He then remarked that he had just had a session with his yoga instructor. Mike then clarified with him whether this was just Hatha yoga. He replied, no, it is a serious yoga class where the instructor directs things into a traditional Hindu session. He told Mike that when the instructor focuses on the Hindu material that he personally chills out and quietly meditates on Jesus. It was ironic that when a different theological matter arose in the conversation this same fellow 'could not go there' while at the same time had no qualms being in a typically straight Hindu-oriented yoga class!

Brooke Boon is an American Christian who came to faith as a qualified yoga teacher. In 2003 she devised what she calls Holy Yoga. It has become quite successful with thousands of people practising it in three different continents and it is embraced in the evangelical culture. It has over eight hundred and fifty teachers globally and is raising international media interest with articles under headings like 'Holy yoga wars: spiritual spat as Christians stake claim to Hindu tradition'.[14] Brooke describes her journey in these terms:

> When I became a Christian I took the idea of surrender seriously. I wanted my entire life to be transformed by my new relationship

with Jesus Christ. I surrendered every part of who I was, all that I did, and all that I loved. I wanted Him to be in charge and that included my yoga practice. I was an avid yoga practitioner and a thriving yoga instructor. I wasn't sure how my yoga practice would fit into my newfound faith, so I started focusing on Jesus while on my mat. I quickly discovered a deep and profound connection with Him that I didn't find anywhere else. I realized that my love for God didn't mean that I had to give up my love for yoga and it made this journey even more meaningful. Before I was a Christian, yoga was merely a physical practice that brought me some sense of peace. But, by incorporating prayer, meditation and scripture, my practice transformed into a worship experience. I learned that anything done to honor God is worship and this new yoga experience allowed me to honor God with my heart, spirit, mind, and body.[15]

As they do various postures – whether sitting still or in various movements stretching legs and arms, abdominal stretches etc. – prayer, praise, music, and meditations are woven together. It would be fair to say that Brooke Boon's Holy Yoga is more moderate and 'tame' and suitable for those anchored in western ways of living when compared to the approach taken by Dom Bede Griffiths.
Many other churches and groups in the west have similar ministries that have reshaped yoga but using different labels. For example, a number of churches including a Baptist church in Knoxville, Tennessee conduct 'Redeemed Yoga'. Others simply adopt the title yoga without reservation. Phileena Heuertz grew up in a conservative Christian tradition and accepted that yoga was taboo. She is now connected to the Christianising of yoga and shared from her perspective:

The longest journey you'll ever make is from the head to the heart. And yoga invites us to make that journey. As I have stayed faithful to the practice, I have grown more acquainted with my body – the temple of the Holy Spirit – and I have grown to love that temple and the One who dwells there. I would argue that yoga has, in fact, made me a better Christian.[16]

Recently, Ross was in Bangkok where a conversation was had between a Naga Church leader and an American missionary in Japan. The conversation turned to the pros and cons of yoga. The Naga leader brought to the conversation both his academic training from Oxford and his cultural experiences of life in India and Asia. The American missionary was working in a student ministry in Japan. The issue is unavoidable and it is global. We simply must have a conversation about how it interacts with all aspects of Christian living and mission.

THINGS TO DO

Reflect on Peter's vision (Acts 10:9-16), and contrast it with Paul's words about being unequally yoked (2 Cor. 6:14-16). Listen to what friends, family and work colleagues have said about their experiences of yoga. In light of the spectrum of case studies, discern in what ways you might use some kind of yoga or bodily postures in your prayer life and that of your local church.

START THE CONVERSATION

1. Your friend at work tells you that she has just enrolled in a yoga class. What would be your response to her?
2. Your local church has been asked to rent its premises to a yoga class, or even to conduct one. What is your response? Discuss the pros and cons with members of your church.
3. In your group discuss why you think people are exploring yoga? What stories can you share about your encounter with yoga?
4. In light of the different case studies above, have a conversation with your friends about where you now stand on yoga.

2
HALLOWE'EN –
Trick, treat or harvest?

How many of us have met a witch? Phil Wyman puts that blunt question to all Christians. Most of us would probably have to say that we haven't. Phil cannot avoid witches because he lives and works as a pastor in Salem, Massachusetts. Salem was the place where witch trials were held in colonial American times, and several people were executed for allegedly being witches. Phil was asked to leave his denomination because he was spotted at a witches' gathering, and it was believed that he had compromised his faith. Funnily enough many of his congregation agreed to join him in exile.[1]

Life in Salem for Phil also means that Hallowe'en is unavoidable. He reveals it is a month-long season, and anywhere from half a million to a million people visit the town. He enjoys the fact that the whole community is so open to interacting:

> What other day of the year will people happily open their doors to a knock from a strangely dressed stranger saying funny things to them? In fact, they will be so happy to see you, they will give you a gift of candy. How often does that happen? You couldn't get that to happen on Christmas Day.[2]

Phil knows that many Christians are understandably disturbed about witches and sometimes believe the worst about them. The negative folklore is pretty strong including the absurdity that they sacrifice 'kittens and babies'. As an evangelical pastor he has found little evidence that witches curse churches and individual Christians. Instead he has found the witches he knows are not devil worshippers but are 'generally kind people who want the world to be a better, more peaceful place'. That's why, he says, 'I do not have to hide on Hallowe'en to pray the darkness away'.

During the month-long season in Salem, Phil and his church 'provide live music on the streets, give away free hot cocoa, free hugs, and will set up booths to offer a variety of spiritual counselling'. He believes that this is an opportunity to genuinely and positively connect with all kinds of people who are on a spiritual search:

> I believe that Halloween is the most open and community oriented holiday in our culture. It is filled with wild creativity, and offers Christianity the best moment in the year to shine with its own creativity, love and giving. Don't let that moment pass you by, because you are afraid of some bogey man of urban myth in fundamentalist garb.[3]

The Scottish theologian John Drane has shared with us his childhood memory of Hallowe'en is of the churches in Scotland having parties along the American lines of kids dressing up, and telling fun spooky stories. In fact the dark folklore side of Hallowe'en has developed over the last thirty years. He believes English and other western churches have been heavily influenced by the spiritual warfare model we outlined in the introduction. As one Lutheran has observed we have shifted to a belief in a dour kill-joy devil, and lost confidence that Christ is in control.

Phil's position is definitely not going to be the same for all. Many feel very strongly that the crass commercialism and Pagan origins make the festival unrecoverable for Christians. No doubt what upsets many of us is the perverse way that everything to do with Hallowe'en is overrun by commercial interests. In most western countries it is now one of the three biggest shopping days and rivals Christmas for its appeal. Sociologists have noted that the child's collection bag of goodies is an icon for the future consumer-shopper at the mall. So much money changes hand with the festivity that it sickeningly reinforces selfish values about me, me, and me. As one Catholic leader has said of the trick or treat ritual:

> As a boy I grew up with the custom in the US, where it was completely harmless and lots of fun for everyone ... What I do not like about it is the fact that it introduces children to what in adults would be called a protection racket: threatening people with harm if they do not pay a sum of money.[4]

A survey in England

A limited qualitative survey was undertaken in two parts of England – London and Lincolnshire. It was among primary school pupils in years two and six. The findings in some respects were quite predictable and not surprising, and corresponded to results found in other global surveys. The survey supplies some interesting insights into what families perceive about this day. It was intriguing to discover the extent to which children from differing backgrounds were participating in Hallowe'en activities.

The survey disclosed that 88.6 per cent of children participate in some way in these activities. Of those surveyed 93 per cent of non-religious pupils, and 74 per cent of religious pupils were actively involved. When the children surveyed used adjectives to describe Hallowe'en, 33per cent called it 'fun-scary' and 19 per cent 'exciting' with just 2 per cent calling it 'boring' and 1 per cent 'dangerous'.

A substantial number of pupils enjoy the festival particularly in receiving treats/gifts (60 per cent), the opportunity to dress up (46 per cent), and meeting friends (11 per cent). It was also noted that the range of activities covers games, walking the streets, parties, dressing up, making pictures, and watching scary movies.

For children dressing up as the latest Disney characters is very much a part of growing up today. Hallowe'en is one festival that really embraces fun. It is also an opportunity for adults to dress up in character and tap into the 'child within'. Also noted from the survey is that the perceptions held by parents and teachers are not necessarily shared by the pupils.[5]

The divide over Hallowe'en is fairly intense among Christians and churches. Do we prohibit it, Christianise it, or just let it be as it is? We will look at the background, discernment, and case studies that come from a variety of approaches.

BACKGROUND

In light of the intense and passionate convictions that are held about Hallowe'en everyone, no matter how pro or anti we are about this festival, needs to take some time to get our facts straight concerning its origins. It is fair to say that in the last twenty to thirty years that a lot of anxiety has developed among Christians who have voiced alarm in various contexts such as youth groups, school boards, and in media campaigns. British historian Ronald Hutton has claimed that evangelicals stick to two basic points: One is that this is a day that glorifies evil; the other is that it is an unchristian festival that is to be opposed because it does not fit in a Christian culture.[6]

It appears that there are really three versions of Hallowe'en – Christian, Pagan, and Secular Commercial.

Christian Hallowe'en

There was a festival that emerged specifically to remember those who had been martyred. The evidence traces back to St Ephrem the Syrian in the fourth century who had a specific day set aside in May for honouring all those who had been martyred by the Roman Emperors. Another kind of festival developed related to commemorating all dead Christians in medieval Europe and the Near East. In Syrian churches the time for this was in Easter week, while in Greek churches it was the Sunday after Pentecost. In Rome the preferred date was in May, and Pope Boniface IV fixed that date in 609.

However, in both England and Germany the practice of

what is called All Soul's Day developed in the ninth century and this was celebrated on 1 November. Other celebration days were celebrated throughout the year in different regions.

What emerges in the liturgical calendar are two days for commemoration. The first is All Saints' Day (1 November) followed by All Souls' Day (2 November). The uniform celebration with the specific naming of All Saints' Day or All Hallows' Eve, is attributed to Pope Gregory IV in 835. He settled the day of observance as 1 November. Hallowe'en simply means Hallows' Eve, where the term Hallow refers to the officially recognised saints. The evening before All Saints' Day is of course the night of 31 October. In classic liturgical practice the various prayers began at sunset and a midnight vigil was held on important feast days (such as Good Friday, Christmas, and All Saints' Day).

In the medieval Catholic system we have the liturgical calendar giving rise to the observance of All Saints Day which refers to all those (including martyrs) who were sanctified and went directly to heaven. The feast of all souls or All Souls' Day was for everyone else who had gone to Purgatory for a time of purging prior to final entry into heaven.

In the Anglican/Church of England, and in other Protestant churches, the liturgical calendar recognises both days for observance. The tradition of All Souls Day is a time for remembering dead family members and friends who are part of the communion of saints or family of God.

We know of liturgical churches that celebrate All Saints' Day where they gather on the night before. The liturgy has a basic structure like this:

- Service commences at 7.30pm
- Hymn honouring all the Saints, which may include a ceremony of lighting incense.
- Sermon on the meaning of All Saints' Day.
- Prayer and hymn
- Lighted candles are distributed.
- A procession – the Procession of Peace – begins led by a

priest, minister or deacons carrying palm leaves and the congregation carrying their candles follow.

- The procession exits the church and marches through the nearby streets as a litany is chanted.
- The procession returns to the church.
- The congregation sings the anthem, 'Oh, how glorious is the Kingdom wherein all the saints rejoice with Christ; they are clothed in white robes; they follow the Lamb whithersoever He goeth.'
- The Magnificat (Luke 1:46-55) is recited.
- A blessing is given, followed by a concluding hymn.

> **The Magnificat**
>
> And Mary said: 'My soul magnifies the Lord and my spirit rejoices in God my Saviour, for he has looked on the humble estate of his servant.' Luke 1:46-48 (ESV)

The above is a skeletal frame and, depending on which tradition one is committed to, there are different kinds of emphases that will be made. One of the important unifying facets of the liturgy is that the anthem draws on the Book of Revelation where the martyrs and saints who have been resurrected are clothed in white garments, a sign of purity and holiness. The liturgy makes the apocalyptic connection from those alive on earth to those who have already died in Christ but now live again at God's throne. What is quite visually striking for the street procession is that the clerics wear robes or gowns. This is not just appropriate with respect to the liturgy but also mirrors 'dressing up' as an integral part of participating in Hallowe'en.

It is worth keeping in mind that today's popular culture has embraced Hallowe'en and instead of referring to saints what is substituted is the 'spooky' element about ghosts and the dead. Beyond Hallowe'en the fascination with apocalyptic themes and death is also expressed in pop culture with the interest in movies and TV shows featuring zombies, werewolves and other undead creatures. The Church has an interesting opportunity when celebrating All Saints' Day and All Souls' Day, and the resurrection of the dead, to creatively link this to the pop cultural interests in the spooky and the Undead. Perhaps other Christian gatherings that do not celebrate these calendar events need to explore the challenge that Hallowe'en offers. One is to reflect on the role of the church year, and then another is to rediscover a robust theology of the resurrection.[7]

Pagan

The origins of a pagan festival are shrouded in some mystery. It is important to exercise some caution here as the historical evidence is quite patchy. There has been much myth-making in the past two hundred years about the ancient Celtic festivals and their links to pre-Christian Paganism. One needs to sift carefully through the claims made about what ritual festivals existed and what they celebrated.

In northern and central Europe and across the British Isles one can find huge variations in the sort of festive activities that were observed. A festival in the highlands of Scotland was not necessarily the same in the lowland regions. Likewise, a festival celebrated in southern Ireland was bound to be very different from one observed in England's northern counties. There is not enough evidence to show that festivals were celebrated everywhere. The cycle picks up fragments found in pre-Christian times through to medieval times, and others occurring in the early modern era of the seventeenth century.

We do know that in some places from pre-Christian times it was customary to celebrate an end of season harvest festival in preparation for the onset of winter in the northern hemisphere. One would have completed reaping the harvest of crops and/or mustered in one's flocks or herds. Some festive activities around a bonfire involved a time for tale-telling about life and dying, which was correlated to the seasonal changes as autumn leads into winter. Winter symbolised a time where nature appeared to 'die'.

Other kinds of folkloric tales were recounted about impish spirits or ghosts that might haunt places. The punch-line would be about being on guard or avoiding such imps.

A festival known from the Gaelic word Samhain (sow-in) gradually emerged and it was understood that a portal could open between the world of the living and the realm of the dead. For some, Samhain became a religious festival to celebrate the Lord of the Dead that coincided with harvest time near the end of autumn. It is known that Irish migrants in the Middle Ages brought to the Scottish highlands the word Samhain, and this is traceable to the seventh century.[8] A harvest festival, which was dubbed Samhain, gradually developed and it seems like local superstitions and folktales were attached to it. It is quite plausible that over time scattered tales prompted rituals to shun or frighten away impish spirits. Rituals such as lighting candles, or leaving gifts to placate the dead, probably became local customs that in time have become more widely accepted. In parts of Scotland nights of mischief that involved pranks being played became customary.

An old Irish custom involved farmers gathering food gifts from villagers in preparation for a bonfire feast. The gift of food was associated with signs of good luck and prosperity (treat for those who gave, and curse/trick for those who did not give). During the nineteenth century the severe potato famines led many Irish people to emigrate and settle in the USA. The custom of trick-or-treat that is associated with Hallowe'en today has its roots among the Irish migrants who believed in these signs of good luck.

There are records in parts of England concerning folkloric fears about marsh lights that led to the creation of the jack-o'-lantern. However, the hollowing out of a vegetable (eventually the choice being the pumpkin) only emerges with Irish migrant influence in both England and America from the mid-nineteenth century onwards. The dressing up in costumes to refer to ghosts, goblins and witches is something that developed in the mid-twentieth century.

In modern times neo-Pagan and witchcraft groups celebrate Samhain as one of eight major festivals in their ritual calendar. This

HALLOWE'EN

is known as 'The Wheel of the Year' and it comprises a series of ritual festivals, known as sabbats, which coincide with equinoxes and seasonal changes. The festivals reflect an eight-episode myth, known as the Wheel of the Year myth, where each festival celebrated represents a particular stage in a grand story about a god and goddess. The Wheel of the Year commences with Samhain and finishes with the autumn equinox (festival of Mabon).

Northern Hemisphere	Date Observed	Southern Hemisphere	Date Observed
Samhain	31 October	Beltane	31 October
Yule/Winter Solstice	21 December	Litha/Summer Solstice	21 December
Oimelc/Imbolc	2 February	Lammas/Lughnasadh	2 February
Ostara/Eostre/ Spring Equinox	21 March	Mabon/ Autumn Equinox	21 March
Beltane	30 April	Samhain	30 April
Litha/Summer Solstice	21 June	Yule/Winter Solstice	21 June
Lammas/Lughnasadh	1 August	Oimelc/Imbolc	1 August
Mabon/Autumn Equinox	21 September	Ostara/Eostre/ Spring Equinox	21 September

In the Wheel of the Year myth the sabbat of Samhain discloses that the goddess is carrying in her womb a child of promise. The child is born at the next sabbat known as Yule (25 December). The child grows up during the time that Nature is full of life through the sabbats that encompass spring and summer. Eventually the child becomes an adult who must contest the power of the Dark Lord of the underworld. In this final sabbat the contest brings about the death and then the rising to new life of this god. In many ways, as we have discussed elsewhere, the Wheel of the Year myth about a virginal goddess and the child of promise who dies and rises again bears uncanny resemblance to the gospel.[9] For the dedicated practitioner of neo-Pagan faith, Samhain is a time where one reflects on living and on dying. However, contrary to a lot of urban rumours, this is not a day where Pagans make sacrifices in some diabolical pact with Satan.

The nineteenth century saw Hallowe'en take shape as a popular annual social phenomenon particularly in North America. It carried forward elements of Pagan belief about the dead and the custom of food and gifts associated with harvests. Admittedly many just dabble in Hallowe'en. Serious Pagan beliefs about the Wheel of the Year and the sabbat of Samhain developed in the thoughts of the pioneers of Neo-Pagan witchcraft faith like Gerald Gardner (1884-1964). The spread of Samhain celebrations accelerated in the late twentieth century as popular accounts were published in books and magazines, and then on Neo-Pagan websites. The most deeply committed Pagan practitioners regard Samhain with the same degree of significance and reverence that Christians have concerning Easter.

Secular commercial

The commercially secular version of Hallowe'en is something that has emerged in the past thirty to forty years. What has developed is the take-over of every facet of Hallowe'en – wearing masks and costumes, gifts of food and confectionery, trick-or-treat door-knocking. The commercial interests have spread through shops and malls so that now it is common to see supermarkets with Hallowe'en merchandise prominently displayed. Of course it should be noted that in some western cities the commercial impact may vary. Philip lives in an area where there is a significant number of migrants, none of whom have a background of relatedness to Hallowe'en. Even though the local supermarket generates a lot of energy trying to promote Hallowe'en, the suburban streets are silent. Ross lives in another part of the same city and the local pub, which is close to a university campus, groans with Hallowe'en festivity.

The commercial take-over of Hallowe'en is no different to what has happened to both Christmas and Easter. The displays of products in shops and malls that are geared around these seasons have mere token gestures concerning any real faith, Pagan or Christian. Probably the Pagans are less defensive about the corporate take-over of Hallowe'en because they can enjoy the frivolity, and are less fussed about people dressing-up and pretending to be witches. In some respects, if the curiosity is awakened then people can always talk to committed Pagans.

CONTACT POINTS

The most obvious contact points with Hallowe'en start with the trick-or-treat door-knock. The celebration of Hallowe'en is found in school curricula in many places, and there are many children's parties. Adults also may be invited to Hallowe'en parties, as well as encountering the commercial version in the shopping malls.

Some of us may be living in an area where there are committed Pagans who are neighbours, like Phil Wyman's experiences in Salem. If you find yourself living in that context you may want to enter into conversations. It can be helpful for fruitful conversations to develop if you have some background understanding about Pagan faith that goes beyond just Hallowe'en, such as their understanding of deity, Jesus, the spiritual value of the natural world.[10] For others there is the likelihood of being invited to attend a liturgy which will seem 'alien' if your faith gathering does not follow a liturgical approach to worship services.

DISCERNMENT

The first crucial issue for discernment is really making sure you know the facts about Hallowe'en. We all need to approach the phenomenon as careful fact-checkers because there is so much discredited and unreliable misinformation on the Internet and in books about the occult. We need to avoid the mistake of accepting information at face-value. This problem has been aggravated by individuals who have made-up stories about their involvement in occult, Satanist and witchcraft groups that have later proven to be a fabrication.[11]

Another approach is the kind of response that would come

from that informal group of Christian novelists called The Inklings – including C. S. Lewis, J. R. R. Tolkien, and Charles Williams whose impact is far-reaching with the success of mythic tales like the Narnia Chronicles and *Lord of the Rings*. We could well imagine how they might connect in their story-telling with Hallowe'en today. On one hand, we can see that both Lewis and Tolkien had no difficulty in using the topic of 'magic' and mythical figures of evil like Sauron the Lord of the Rings and the white witch of Narnia in their stories. Charles Williams' last novel was called *All Hallows' Eve*, and it dealt with the interactions between the living and the dead.

On the other hand, Williams took the subject of evil and occultism seriously, and while he was known to enjoy frivolity he would always offer cautionary advice for those who felt the attractive tug toward occult power. In a similar way Tolkien, as a very conservative Catholic, was not happy about people who did not take the occult and evil seriously. His attitude is best summed up in the words he penned in *Lord of the Rings* about the wizard Saruman. The great error of Saruman is that he studied the dark arts of Lord Sauron so closely that he found himself 'hooked' and became a pawn of Mordor.

C. S. Lewis may have found children's fascination with Hallowe'en interesting. Perhaps he would invite everyone to consider his twofold advice in *The Screwtape Letters*:

> There are two equal and opposite errors into which our race can fall about the devils. One is to disbelieve in their existence. The other is to believe, and to feel an excessive and unhealthy interest in them. They themselves are equally pleased by both errors and hail a materialist or a magician with the same delight.[12]

Martin Luther, the father of the Reformation, took the devil seriously as seen in his classic hymn 'A Mighty Fortress is our God'[13] but never allowed himself to fall into the trap of making the devil too big. He was known for his earthy remarks and for laughing at the devil with his taunting words, 'devil you can kiss my ass'.[14]

A Mighty Fortress is our God – Martin Luther

'Though devils all the world should fill,
  all eager to devour us.
We tremble not, we fear no ill,
  they shall not overpower us.
This world's prince may still scowl fierce as he will,
He can harm us none,
  he's judged; the deed is done;
One little word can fell him.'

Some Lutheran colleagues say that we should not settle for a kill-joy devil but rather laugh at him on Hallowe'en and enjoy the good things of the day and share the gospel!

They pray that we don't lose the plot and exaggerate his role and power. They remind us that Christ is victorious and evil powers have been defeated by the cross and resurrection: 'He (Jesus) disarmed the rulers and authorities and put them to open shame, by triumphing over them in him' (Col. 2:15). Their advice is about having confidence in Christ and not ending up with a devil that is too big.

The spiritual warfare model is often more cautious. The scriptural evidence relied on (Deut. 13:1-5; 18:9; Gal 5:19-21; 1 John 4:1-4) does remind us to be wary of being deceived. Discernment means we all walk a fine line and we should maintain an even-handed understanding as expressed in Lewis' advice. If we tie together misinformation with the spiritual warfare model we can end up demonising everything. If we go too far in down-playing the possibility of spiritual deception, then our discernment will also suffer from a failure to be ever-watchful.

As with yoga the same three responses can emerge – prohibit, Christianise, or leave it as it is. There probably are occasions when we may feel inclined to prohibit. This may be necessary when one is placed in situations where children have been 'obliged' to dress-up as witches for Hallowe'en at school. We have personal experiences of cases where a conversation between a parent and teacher to allow a child to have an alternative costume, whether it is an angel or a character out of *Frozen*, was derided and dismissed. If the teacher's narrative is inflexible and narrowly refers to Hallowe'en as a fun or Pagan celebration while ignoring the wider story about its origins as we have told above, then one may genuinely decide not to participate. The same thing may occur in adult contexts where the obligation is to only be in fancy-dress of an evil or wicked character. Again, this can occur when the narrative is limited.

For some of us the commercial stench on its own may be sufficient to warrant a veto for ourselves, or for our whole family. For many of us this has no impact and we leave the commercial version as it is. Whatever your response to Hallowe'en never lose sight of the importance of explaining its background to children. Children appreciate knowing what is good, what may be harmful, and finding balance in things that are fun. It is also a time for addressing the excesses of greed and how instead we can give to others. There are plenty of costumes to dress up in that are not contentious for this time of year. When their friends wear a witch's costume it does not mean that they believe in the occult but, like playing the game of 'cops and robbers,' they enjoy working through what is good and what is evil.

CASE STUDIES

The first kind of response is where Christians who treasure the traditional church calendar simply reassert the primacy of celebrating All Saints' Day. In some respects this might be regarded as 'reclaiming' the day where prayer, hymns, rituals and processions centre on thanking God for Christian martyrs and those who are among the cloud of witnesses (Heb. 12:1; Rev. 6:9). It is possible to simply celebrate All Saints' Day as we do any other important event – Christmas, Easter, Pentecost, etc. – irrespective of what other people are doing on Hallowe'en in secular and Pagan contexts. We have given an illustration of the liturgy.

A second response is where Christians who are not accustomed to celebrating All Saints' Day and do not really follow most of the traditional church calendar, may decide to create an alternative kind of celebration. A few examples include Halo-een and Light Parties. Halo-een has been developed by a colleague of ours, Vanessa Hal, who runs International Trust Ministry. She took the step to launch an alternative in 2012, and she has created some resources, a website, video, and merchandise, themed around love.[15] Vanessa urges Christians to step away from being judgmental of those who choose to celebrate Hallowe'en. She started this ministry as a positive response to Hallowe'en because, in the process of her growth as a Christian, she found herself being reminded of her past cultic involvement in it. Her approach is to empower us and churches to have a different presence and voice on the day. Families wear white costumes or those of angels, adorn their letter boxes with white balloons, and distribute treats like heart-shaped chocolates and Bible verse cards.

Over the past five years in the UK, Australia and elsewhere Light Parties is another trend. Sometimes a local church or a network of churches sponsors a Light Party. The event typically awards prizes for those who come as the best dressed superhero or cartoon character. It features lights as a sign that Jesus is the light of the world and overcomes the darkness. At the party there are all kinds of amusements such as rides, games, craft exercises, giant slides and bouncy castles. Often a Hallowe'en fact sheet is handed out, which briefly covers what we've outlined as the three versions. Scripture Union UK has created on its website an article on alternatives to Hallowe'en, and another page offering resources to use at such parties.[16] It also explores what a Christian light party might look like. The focus is on transition from darkness to light. You might start in a dark space and a Bible story like the Fall, and then physically move around to a new space where the light of Jesus becomes clear. It can include a moment of prayer and remembrance of loved ones who have died.

There are other similar responses from some churches such as Hallowe'en community days which focus on craft, food, and kids' activities. On these occasions the 'true' meaning of Hallowe'en is shared about the hope we have in the resurrected Christ.

A third response is for those Christians who intend to treat Hallowe'en as an opportunity for missional outreach. An example is Columbia Baptist Church in Virginia, which is just a few miles from Washington DC. One of us shared in this church's Hallowe'en outreach. The senior minister, Jim Baucom, is a leader of the Missional Alliance, and he entered into the spirit of the night. It was a 'trunk or treat' Hallowe'en where some 200 cars were parked on the church grounds, and the car trunks or boots were open. Each trunk contained different things like sweets, cakes, toys, prizes, as well as information to support charities. The church members stood by their vehicles dressed up as Disney or superhero characters. There was a barbecue with food served to literally thousands of people from the local community. All the adjacent church doors were open and various spaces inside had a popcorn dispenser, games, face-painting, photographs with 'superheroes'. It was a seamless move from the car park and car trunks to inside the church. People were available to have conversations about faith, and the role of the church in the community. It all worked well.

US pastor Mike Jones moved to Australia in 2004 and has brought to a church culture that is alarmed by Hallowe'en the trunk or treat alternative. On the preceding Sunday he challenged the congregation, 'Some of you may be concerned about what we are going to do if some kids come dressed as gruesome creatures, devils, vampires or witches. Well if that's the case and it probably will be, we are going to let them in, love them, be gracious to them and care for them.' His small Lakeside Baptist Church, with a Sunday school of twenty-five children, connected to one hundred and eighty children in the Hallowe'en outreach. Three hundred people attended the BBQ and the majority were unchurched. The programme was similar to the one above. As one grandparent said, 'I just can't believe the church just cares for our families so much that you would do all of this.'

If we discern it is appropriate there are various ways that we can make a connection to Hallowe'en. Perhaps the provocative question we need to consider is, should this event stay as it is? Or is it possible to make the event less ghoulish and less commercial, and turn it into something very positive?

THINGS TO DO

Take an inventory of Hallowe'en activities in your neighbourhood. Consider what other Churches and Christian groups are doing. Is your neighbourhood featuring more Pagan spirituality, more of a fancy-dress party or more commercial trick-or-treat? Ponder what you and/or your local church might do for the next year's celebration. Reflect on Phil. 4:8 and ask in what ways the experience of Hallowe'en in the lives of your friends and neighbours is consistent or inconsistent with the message of this text.

START THE CONVERSATION

1. Your child's school or office holds a Hallowe'en party that everyone is expected to attend. How would you engage in a conversation with this school about the meaning of Hallowe'en?
2. Your friends are considering an alternative to Hallowe'en trick-or-treat where their house is decorated for Christmas and they hand out gifts and a message about all the calendar events. What would your response be?
3. Your local church is considering a plan to undertake a future event scheduled for Hallowe'en. In your group consider the range of case studies and what your advice would be?

4. Think of a friend or relative who enjoys Hallowe'en in either a Pagan or commercial sense. How would you start a conversation with them about Hallowe'en?
5. Scripture Union UK has the following quote on its website: 'Even those who for fun get involved in astrology, séances and spells risk devastating consequences. They're unleashing forces on their lives they don't understand and often can't combat.' Talk about this claim with your friends and mentors and find out if you agree or disagree with this quote.

3
AROMATHERAPY –
Sacred oils or spirits?

Today touch and scent are part of the lifestyle experiences of many of us. Aromatherapy is a complementary therapy that uses oils or essences extracted from plants to assist in healing and well-being. The oils are primarily applied through bathing, massage or by inhaling the scents. It is easy to access as it is used in hospital clinics and therapeutic massage centres. In some countries it is part of the National Health Service for purposes of medical rebates.[1] Aromatherapy is also offered as a health and well-being treatment for dogs and cats. The value and testability of aromatherapy is discussed in various health professional journals, including some published by Christian medical practitioners. There are many happy customer stories in health magazines, and the oils can be bought at the local chemist. Aromatherapy is a popular healing technique that many people swear by, as evidenced by neighbourhood parties showcasing the products and benefits.

We have met various practitioners of aromatherapy, some are committed to alternative spiritual beliefs, others are pragmatists, and some are followers of Jesus. The same categories apply among those who consume and enjoy the therapy. Some people are adamant about 'why' the oils 'work'.

The claim that aromatherapy is a spiritual holistic tool that can heal our bodies, our minds and our spirits is far reaching. For example, we have spoken in churches and community groups in several countries and it is not unusual to encounter distressed Christian students in massage and beautician classes who have stories about what they have been taught. In some tertiary settings the course instructors have taught them theories about bush spirits or forces of energy and claim that these sources actually activate the healing properties of the oils. The struggle for these students has been about discernment, particularly the binary choice of 'to do or taboo'.

On the one hand, students have faced the difficult pressure of completing the course/workshop because their employer has paid for the training. On the other hand, there is the practical and undeniable fact that in many ways aromatherapy appears to work. Is its effectiveness a matter of pure science? Or is it due to some spiritual power or energy?

Many of the questions that arise in studying aromatherapy, also apply to other healing modalities.

BACKGROUND

The use of oils extracted from plants is not new as anyone who studies ancient near eastern cultures will tell you: the use of 'medical botany' is quite old. Aromatic scents and oils were used in the biblical world in a holistic way in the passages of life, worship, eating, gifts and trade.

We sometimes forget that oils and essences were used in the Bible and that may be because some references to them are in those 'least-read' bits of the Old Testament connected to the tabernacle and temple. It is interesting to see how oils were routinely used in ritual worship. Israel's ancestor, Jacob, poured oil over two stone memorials that he set up after his visions (Gen. 28:18-22; 35:14). The process of using oils in acts of worship continued when Israel left Egypt. The priests consecrated the sacred utensils that they used in the tabernacle and temple (Exod. 40:9-11). Oils were used in ceremonial offerings of praise (Exod. 25:6; 29:38-42; 30:22-38; Numbers 28:3-6). Tithes (Ezekiel 45:25), first-fruit offerings to God in harvests (Deut. 18:4), and food offerings at the tabernacle/temple were often mixed with oil or had it poured over them (Exod. 29:40; Lev. 2:1; Numbers 28:5; Ezekiel 45:24). They were also used in the purification offerings for those who were declared to be free from leprosy (Lev. 14:10). The anointing oil was extracted from plants such as olives and spices, like aromatic cane, myrrh and cinnamon (Exod. 30:22-25).

Another important sacred ritual involved anointing kings where oil was used as an external sign that God's Spirit rested on them (1 Sam. 10:1; 16:3; 1 Kings 1:39; 2 Kings 9:6 cf. Isa. 61:3). A similar anointing ceremony involved using oil on priests consecrated for service (Exod. 29:7; Lev. 8:12; 21:10). In other contexts, oil was used for lighting and in cooking food (Exod. 25:6; 27:20; Matt. 25:3). It was used as toiletries (Ruth 3:3; 2 Sam. 12:20), and in perfuming garments (Ps. 45:8; Prov. 7:17). Oil was a hospitable sign of welcome for guests (Luke 7:46). Oils were traded as commodities (2 Kings 4:7; 2 Chronicles 2:10; Rev. 18:13) and, were also used in various close family relationships in relaxation and love-making (Song of Songs 3:6; 4:6, 11; 5:1, 5, 13).

Significant symbolism was attached to oils. They were symbols of joy (Ps. 45:8; Heb. 1:9), and could signify wisdom when used appropriately (Prov. 21:17, 20). They were also linked to fellowship and friendship (Ps. 133:1-2) and the restoration of strength (Ps. 92:10).

Oils are sometimes described as medicinal healing aids (Isa. 1:6; Luke 10:34). The story of the Good Samaritan describes his practical assistance to the man who had been beaten and left for dead. We learn that the Good Samaritan bound up the man's wounds and applied both oil and wine as a healing aid to the wounds. In Isaiah the prophet refers to Israel by way of the metaphor of having a human body that has sore feet and raw wounds. Isaiah indicates that oil was clearly a soothing or healing agent applied to sore skin and wounds but, as he was addressing Israel, the nation's sinful sores remained unhealed. In a different context we read that oil was used in the healing ministry of the church (James 5:14). It is not clear from the text if this was merely a symbolic rite or if it was also being used as a curative aid. It is possible that it could have been used in both ways.

The gifts to Jesus at his birth include myrrh and frankincense (Matt. 2:11). Jesus was anointed with expensive oil shortly before his arrest and crucifixion (Matt. 26:6-13; Mark 14:3-9; John 12:1-8), and used in preparing his body for burial (Matt. 26:12; Luke 23:56; John 19:40). The act of anointing is specifically linked to the announcing of the gospel (Isa. 61:3; Luke 4:18-21).

In medieval times Christian monastics practised botanic healing, and one respected authority was the twelfth-century abbess Hildegard of Bingen who wrote on the topic. In the wake of the Reformation, there were Christian naturalists like Caspar Bartholin, Leonard Fuchs and Christian Torkelsen Morsing who taught medical botany at Lutheran universities. Some Christian physicians in England, including John Ray and Nehemiah Grew, published textbooks on medical botany. What church history shows is that the monks and nuns, and the medical teachers who used oils and potions extracts from herbs and other plants, all gave glory to God for these natural elements found in God's creation.

It is quite clear from the wide range of Bible verses that using oils extracted from plants was a normal daily experience in the days of Israel and when Jesus walked the earth. Oils had 'sacred' functions when used in the tabernacle/temple, in healing, and in anointing ceremonies. They also had 'ordinary' uses in daily life. Nobody attached any sense of the oils being a source of evil, although like anything else in the creation they could be corruptly misused for idolatrous purposes. What is clear is that the oils had a sacred purpose as a direct link, by way of symbol and ceremony, to God's Spirit.

Alternate spiritualities

The modern day technique that we call aromatherapy stems from the work of the French perfumer Rene-Maurice Gattefossé. He coined the term aromatherapy in 1937. Gattefossé was largely concerned about the medicinal uses of the oils.[2] Others who followed in his wake began to expand the theories behind aromatherapy, and some theorists made explicit links to a spiritual paradigm.

One early pioneer was Marguerite Maury, a trained nurse. She studied Zen Buddhism, yoga, macrobiology and naturopathy. She formed the view that your body could regenerate using the oils, and she explained that practitioners may do this by accessing a 'life force' or 'vital energy':

> When we are dealing with an essential oil and its odoriferance, we are dealing directly with a vital force and entering the very heart of the alchemy of creation.[3]

Maury did not hesitate to explain 'why' aromatherapy works in terms of a spiritual worldview. Many practitioners like Maury believe that the human body is more than just a physical entity. It is claimed that humans and non-human creatures possess a 'subtle anatomy' where we have five different layers or bodies: the physical, etheric, astral, mental, and causal. Each of the bodies beyond the physical is invisible to the naked eye but they may be detected by a skilled practitioner. If you wish your physical body wears like a glove the other bodies.

The fivefold concept of the body is drawn out of Hindu belief and has been adapted by classic teachers of New Age/alternative spiritualities like Charles Leadbeater. The etheric and astral bodies are connected to the spiritual realm and it is believed that one can use these bodies to enter or travel through spiritual places of the universe. This is sometimes known as astral travel where, in an altered state of consciousness like a trance or dream, this invisible body may drift freely to higher spiritual realms or to other galaxies.

Inside the mental body are those energy centres that are known to us in yoga as chakras, and chakras are discussed in our chapter on yoga. A few clarifying words though about chakras and aromatherapy may be helpful. The chakras as energy centres in our anatomy may be activated like switching on an electric light through meditation. While we explain the energy paradigm in detail in the next chapter, it is helpful to know that 'energy' is associated with a concept called the 'universal life force' which is believed to fill everything in the universe. In this mystical understanding of energy the claim is made that we are all connected to divine energy, and the view of God in this outlook is known as 'all is one' or 'all is god'.

The heart chakra is associated with essences of rose, inula, bergamot and jasmine. When these essences are massaged into that chakra the invisible vibrations are activated to bring about healing. In the broad theory about chakras and our bodies, we become unwell when our energetic harmony is out of balance with the whole cosmos. In order to restore wellness, we must reharmonize the flow of this energy through our physical, etheric, astral, mental and causal bodies.

We discovered that a Church of England high school was the venue for a ten week evening course in aromatherapy. This piqued our interest. The facilitator outlined the weekly course content which looked very attractive with lessons on bath products, foot products, facial therapy and skin care. What drew our attention though was the first week's class syllabus. It included an overview of the course and learning goals but also set out the theory and beliefs associated with 'Holism and the Chakras'.[4] Although this was clearly offered as an Adult Education programme to the community, we were intrigued that there had apparently been 'no questions asked' or no concerns expressed by the school authorities prior to hiring out their property to the course facilitator.

Other practitioners believe in a somewhat different model to chakras that nevertheless has a concept of universal energy. The classic Chinese theory of the way the universe operates is taught in the philosophy of Taoism ('Dowism'). Taoists refer to a concept that is called Chi or Qi. In this model the human body may be mapped out as having energy points which are called meridians. Chi or Qi flows through our body and illnesses develop when our Chi energy is unbalanced. This balance may be restored by working on the meridians to remove blockages to the flow of Chi.

What has impressed students, consumers and those who are practitioners of aromatherapy is that these models of energy appear to be validated in western science. The claim is made that what Einstein discovered about atomic matter provides proof that everything in the material universe consists of energy in different forms. What is stated in some popular aromatherapy textbooks is that the terms energy, vital force, and universal life force are synonyms for God. In these texts God is an impersonal being. We will set to one side the energy paradigm and discuss the discernment issues about it in the next chapter.

What we will now concentrate on in this chapter is the direct association that some practitioners make between occult practices like astrology, bush spirits and animal spirit guides and the effectiveness of the properties of the oils. The word occult refers to the secret or hidden things, and is typically associated with beliefs and practices that are outside the religious mainstream and may be linked to external spiritual powers or spirits. Some Christians use the term very broadly and apply it to beliefs and practices regarded as demonic in origin.

One reason why aromatherapy is considered to have occult connections is that some practitioners combine it with things like astrology. In an astrological version of aromatherapy the position of planets in the constellations plays a key part in the diagnosis of an illness. It may also be important for aligning specific oils as a suitable remedy to the influence of a planet in your zodiac sign. For example, Venus is the planet of love and for the skin. Venus' influence links to herbs of love including the rose and geranium.[5]

The vocabulary common to believers in occult powers sometimes turns up in the literature. Kurt Schnaubelt is one leading American practitioner who introduces the topic by stating that 'Aromatherapy is shamanism for everyone'.[6] A shaman is a figure in tribal cultures who is able to mediate between the tribe and the world of spirits. In colloquial terms a shaman is the old 'witch doctor'.

Scott Cunningham is committed to Neo-Pagan spirituality and he advocates a magical version of aromatherapy. He instructs that the use of mind powers to create one's reality are valuable: 'visualization is maintained while inhaling the fragrance of aromatic plant materials or essential oils'.[7]

There are practitioners who believe that aromatherapy works

best when we understand the bush spirits that activate the healing properties of oils. A bush spirit is an invisible being or entity that is directly linked to a particular plant or species of plants. This idea is very much part of an animist understanding of reality where the cosmos is populated by all kinds of spirits that have powers to make all sorts of things in the natural world 'work'. Some take this a step further and maintain that we may inhale aromatic scents for healing while simultaneously seeking an animal spirit guide. Aletheia Luna has discussed five aromatherapy oils one may use to invoke animal spirit guides. She recommends that if your life's circumstances are troubled by a lack of compassion, meaning, relationship difficulties, financial instability or career problems, then one may try a ritual to make contact with an animal spirit that could appear in a dream, a vision or while meditating. For example, the lotus flower thrives in water and can connect us with aquatic spirit guides such as the seahorse, salmon, frog, octopus, and shark.[8]

Secular aromatherapy

Many consumers and practitioners of aromatherapy do not share in the spiritual convictions outlined above. Some people are highly pragmatic and use essential oils in massage and by inhalation without holding to any spiritual beliefs. Others accept that 'it works' and have no interest in the energy paradigm or occult spirit paradigm but may incline to the view that aromatherapy has justification because of the basic facts of chemistry. Yet again there are those who may view the oils as one of God's gifts but not hold to an alternate spirituality worldview. The latter may include Christians.

It should be apparent though that there are some prominent theorists of aromatherapy from its earliest development who do hold to a spiritual worldview, and the roots of that may be traced back to either a spirit-based belief or a mystical energy-based paradigm.

TWO POPULAR THERAPIES

Homeopathy:
Samuel Hahneman (1755-1843) was a German doctor who developed homeopathy. He was a follower of Emmanuel Swedenborg's teachings. As a system of treatment, homeopathy operates on the basis that like cures like. The remedies prescribed are in very small dosages, because Hahneman believed that a prescription is most effective when diluted. The dilution process is necessary to activate the spiritual energy or universal life force latent in the remedy.

Naturopathy:
Naturopathy rejects the germ theory of disease. Instead, disease arises from the accumulation of toxins and waste products inside the body. Treatments focus on cleansing the body of such toxins so that the body can heal itself. Remedies encompass acupuncture, aromatherapy, breathing exercises, colon cleansing, exercise, fasting, herbs, massage, reflexology, and vitamin supplements.

Some work within a Christian belief system, others have no spiritual beliefs, while others incline towards alternate spiritual beliefs about the universal life force.

CONTACT POINTS

There are different contexts in which we may encounter aromatherapists and people exploring aromatherapy. Beyond those we have mentioned above, chaplains might encounter this in hospitals, hospices, and aged care facilities. Others will certainly encounter practitioners in alternate spiritual festivals and exhibitions. It may turn up in health-care studies at a college or university. We have been asked questions about it in church gatherings where parishioners have family members who are trying aromatherapy for relaxation or as an adjunct to other medical treatments. Aromatherapy is a good conversation starter on matters to do with God, healthy lifestyles, and healing.

DISCERNMENT

Many people will swear that lavender really does work in relaxing and calming. There are many anecdotes that circulate about the beneficial use of aromatherapy oils in a bath, or in a massage that is helpful and invigorating. Our interactions with members of Christian medical and nursing fellowships go further. There are obvious signs where it works in perfumes, as antiseptics, respiratory tract decongestants, fumigation, and pain relief.

These same medical people often urge one to be very cautious where extravagant claims are made in the absence of careful clinical tests where practitioners suggest that aromatherapy will cure diseases. It is always wise to check for proper evidence rather than just relying on personal endorsements. Many Christian medical practitioners also share in the kinds of reservations mentioned above over worldviews that lead to spirits or mystical energy claims.[9] There are all kinds of clinical trials that have been conducted to demonstrate that the use of oils may help alleviate agitation among certain kinds of patients suffering from dementia. In other trials cancer patients in palliative care have found that anxieties lessen when oils are used in massage therapy. Other studies indicate that moods may change in a positive calming way, stress reduction and changes in brain wave patterns.[10] In a recent documentary, the doctor behind the '5:2 diet' Michael Moseley was conducting supervised university trials which included the inhaling of rosemary. To his surprise the trials with respect to rosemary pointed to the improvement of memory. He admitted his cynicism with respect to aromatherapy was challenged.[11]

AROMATHERAPY

In general we should keep in mind that aromatherapy is as much about the *practitioner's worldview* as it is about the practice. We talked with a colleague whose daughter had a medical complaint that was resistant to mainstream medical treatment. She then used the services of a practitioner of an alternate healing method which, in terms of consumer acceptance, is very mainstream, and in various respects resembles aromatherapy. Her complaint was successfully brought under control, so there was no doubt that the treatment 'worked'. The intriguing thing is that the practitioner passed on to her a copy of a book that explained his healing philosophy. There was no mistaking the worldview as being based not on 'pure science', but rather on a mystical occult belief. The worldview was shaping his entire approach to healing and in interacting with patients.

We posed the question to our colleague, 'what might happen to your daughter the next time she has a difficult medical problem? If she relies on this practitioner and finds it once again is helpful, is it not likely that she will want to explore or follow his worldview?'

When we have had conversations with practitioners of aromatherapy and other healing practices, we have found it beneficial to consider these general principles of discernment:

- Be open to healing. A wise principle is that nothing is inherently evil and medical alternatives may be explored.
- Avoid excessive drug treatments. The body is to be the temple of the Holy Spirit.
- Seek healing by means of natural remedies where possible. Diet, herbs and relaxation are examples of this.
- See diet in the framework of spiritual significance. Some pertinent texts to meditate on include the miracle feeding of the 5,000, Jesus' last supper, and the marriage supper of the lamb (Rev. 19:7-9).
- Stay in touch with reality and do not simplify the causes of illness. Diseases as an illusion or as the result of my thought patterns are two examples of such oversimplification.

- Read widely before experimenting. Test the spirits.
- If in doubt, check it out! This is a useful and ancient common-sense principle.[12]

Depending on your particular tradition, you may want to delve further as an exercise in discernment. Ruth Pollard is a Christian legal apologist who engages in market-place outreach. She has studied the connection points between the Bible and aromatherapy, and advises that we should keep in mind these points when considering the services of a practitioner:

- The principal creators of aromatherapy were committed to particular world-views, either built on a mystic energy concept or drawn from occult beliefs and practices such as astrology, and the Kabbalah, or on the existence of bush spirits.
- Several practitioners do emphasise the bush spirits and claim that they are activating or manipulating such forces. At this juncture, Christians should pause and consider if this brings us to the threshold of deception. It is also important to reflect that spiritually immature Christians might involuntarily stumble if they witness other Christians using something that seems to be heavily rooted in occult practices.
- Aromatherapy usually involves extracting oils from plants, which in itself is spiritually neutral. However, there are practitioners who claim that the reason why the distilled oil 'works' is due to the 'universal life force' in the plant. The practitioner who claims there is a universal life force is basically making a philosophical point which is linked to a pantheist understanding of reality – the belief that 'all is god'. The occult belief that there is a universal life force in plants is *sometimes* expressed by people who advocate macrobiotic, fruitarian and vegan diets.

CASE STUDIES

A very high percentage of visitors to the alternate spirituality festivals who find aromatherapy and massage appealing are women. A model that we have seen operate in these contexts is where an exhibitor's booth offers aromatherapy foot washing where extracted oils come as the form of a cream lotion, or are diluted in warm water, and are massaged as a skin cleanser. Since visitors seeking a foot massage are mostly female, it is an appropriate protocol to only have women providing the hands-on massage. The booth can be decorated in an overtly Christian manner with a cross on display, and also offering a prayer-chair. Since there is ample evidence of the use of oils in the Bible, the booth may make good connections in its visual displays back to appropriate scriptures.

The process of the foot massage takes some time and the experience creates a space for a conversation to unfold. This may lead the providers of the massage to simply listen or, where appropriate, to share their own faith-story. We have witnessed in numerous cases the conversations do reach a point where the recipient of the massage is open to

Five most mentioned oils in the Bible
• Myrrh
• Frankincense
• Cedarwood
• Cinnamon
• Cassia

prayer. It is helpful to distribute leaflets or other kinds of literature that outline the biblical uses of oils (like the material set out earlier in this chapter).

This particular approach is adaptable to a variety of settings beyond the festivals, and may be conducted in a church building as part of a healing service. In an age where healing services play a part, such as the Order of St Luke, the biblical association of oils with healing may broaden the mode of interacting. It can be transferred into other public venues and it is not resource intensive.

In a healing service one might go beyond merely a symbolic

making of the sign of the cross on a person's forehead. A more expansive approach involves drawing on some of the most popular oils and personalising their use to each individual's prayer requests. The popular oils on sale today include lavender, peppermint, eucalyptus, and chamomile. We have previously mentioned the role of lavender, and of oils in the context of decongestants. In a ceremonial approach one might draw attention to Frankincense due to its use in promoting a sense of calm and enhancing or boosting immunity.

We have met Christian aromatherapists who promote their business via house parties. The facilitator speaks about the spiritual significance of oils in the birth, death, burial and resurrection of Jesus. They encourage people to use the products wisely and sample them at the party.

It is also possible to run an 'open house' gathering on the Bible and oils along the lines of explaining the role of oils in scripture for healing and worship.[13] In Asia we have met Christian aid workers who have employed survivors of prostitution and people trafficking to manufacture products that contain lavender or other essential oils in candles and soaps with appropriate healing mottoes like 'Jesus heals', 'God's love heals' etc.

There is another forum where one may interact with the general public and that is via a radio broadcast. This may work well in either a community or a mainstream radio station. One of us did exactly this for fifteen years on radio and was quite popular among a broad listening audience. This operates well with a two or three person panel to discuss aromatherapy and to answer questions from listeners who phone the show. The best way this works is where a qualified medical practitioner who is open to using some complimentary healing techniques is able to answer health questions, while another panellist is a chaplain or pastor who may also address health and healing from a spiritual/counselling angle. When listeners call, conversations may take all sorts of directions and can lead to prayer on the air.

The use of oils and essences for our well-being is not foreign to biblical Christianity. 'Taboo or to do?' remains a question when one considers whether the aromatherapy practitioner is clearly linked to bush spirits and other sources. Also, can aromatherapy from these origins evolve beyond its roots?

THINGS TO DO

Check out your local community for practitioners and well-being centres that offer aromatherapy and other complementary healing practices. Convene a workshop to discover what pool of talent exists in your church gathering and neighbouring churches of people who have training or skills in these areas. Consider ways in which your gathering/group might creatively interact with the wider community on the biblical understanding of oils, healing and well-being.

START THE CONVERSATION

1. 'Another important sacred ritual involved anointing kings where oil is used as an external sign that God's Spirit rested on them' (1 Sam. 10:1; 16:3; 1 Kings 1:39; 2 Kings 9:6 cf. Isa. 61:3). Take time to read and discuss the meaning of these passages. Does your group/gathering ever perform rituals using oils as a sign that God's Spirit rests on us in ministry? If not, why not?

2. In your group reflect on the other biblical passages about oils, and discuss how oils may be applied to our lives for relaxation, health and well-being.

3. If possible try to have a conversation with a practitioner of aromatherapy and/or other complimentary therapies. Explore with the practitioner how they see their role as a healer, listener, pastoral carer, in relation to their clients and the community. Is this a case where the practitioner is taking over a role that was once undertaken by priests or ministers in the community?

4
ENERGY HEALING (REIKI, ACUPUNTURE) –
Mystic power or God's Spirit?

We were recently watching cable TV network news. A regular 'health report' segment is one of our favourite spots. This segment featured, in a very positive light, the work of a practitioner of energy healing. It said that her fingers have the magic touch. The healer's practice was warmly endorsed by football stars, bankers, and film producers. The emphasis was on her holistic healing tool-box and the segment directed attention to the healer's website.

The holistic healing tool-box included: aromatherapy, Eden Energy Medicine, Emotional Freedom Technique, crystals, and muscle activation technique. Eden Energy Medicine and muscle activation technique involves the practitioner channelling universal energy into the body to effect healing. The Emotional Freedom Technique involves acupressure where, instead of needles, fingertip pressure is applied. At the conclusion of the segment the show's reporter said 'We must get some of that!' It was stated that some of these eastern healing methods can nicely complement western medicine. There were no critical points raised in the segment but rather it was accepted at face-value that energy healing is wholesome and good.

A common understanding here is that all matter in the universe consists of energy that exists in different material forms, such as light, rocks, sand, trees, bodily flesh. It is a fundamental belief among energy healers that our bodies experience imbalances in the natural flow of invisible energy. When imbalances occur we experience either acute (short-term) or chronic illnesses. The way to restore health and well-being is through channelling energy into the body and removing blockages. Many people now understand that all parts of their bodies are interconnected, and massaging a blockage in one part of the body may bring relief to other parts of the body. A deep sense of wholeness is also felt in mind and body when illnesses are gone. There are two principal approaches that both rely on the use of our hands. In some energy healing methods the hands are directly laid on the body to transmit energy, while in other methods the hands are not placed on the patient's body but rather hover just above it.

Energy healing methods are taught in some nurses' training courses. It is quite mainstream in its use and acceptance, and it can be accessed in healing centres in the community. A friend of ours is the CEO of a major Christian provider for aged care. She contacted us and asked should she endorse the Reiki programme that was being used in her facilities. She said it was popular with the residents who were at a stage of life where the experience of touch and care of tired bodies is treasured. We stressed that such care is important to us as a Christian agency. Nondenominational chaplains had personally contacted her raising their concerns.

BACKGROUND

The use of human hands in healing is very ancient and also features in the Bible. The prophets or apostles acted in ways similar to those of Jesus when meeting distressed and seriously ill individuals. They would touch the people and speak or pray (2 Kings 4:34; John 9:6-7; Acts 9:17). As a physiotherapist recently said to us that the two key elements that shape medicine and healing today are appropriate physical touch and listening. This insight ultimately harks back to the biblical world where both touch and listening were combined with words of prayer. The New Testament neatly describes the apostles' ministry in these words:

> So they remained for a long time, speaking boldly for the Lord, who bore witness to the word of his grace, granting signs and wonders to be done by their hands. (Acts 14:3 ESV)

One of the amazing visionary experiences in the Bible is where the prophet Habakkuk sees God:

> His splendour covered the heavens, and the earth was full of his praise. His brightness was like the light; rays flashed from his hand; and there he veiled his power. (Hab. 3:3-4)

This passage has prompted our friends in the Eastern Orthodox Church to speak about our being immersed in the energies of God that fill the whole creation. A connection between divine energy and hands is apparent in scripture and in such theological reflections.

However the energy healing that is discussed earlier is not scripturally focused. There are diverse views about the source of this energy, how it is accessed, and used to heal. The diagram below refers to several different versions of energy healing, and some theories that have shaped the arguments to support its validity.

Contributing Methods and Ideas to Energy Healing

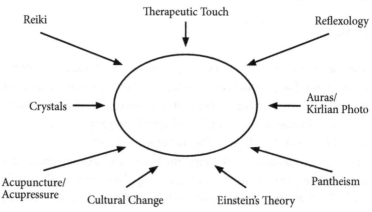

ENERGY HEALING

Einstein's theory

Many healers claim that energy healing is supported by Einstein's theory which states that at a sub-atomic level energy never dies but just changes form. Western practitioners have jumped from that insight to maintain that they can access universal energy and channel it into our bodies to bring about healing from illnesses. Donna Eden, who is a pioneer of energy healing in the west, expresses it this way:

> While our culture does little to help us look more closely, energy *really* is all there is. Even matter, as Einstein's elegant formula shows, is congealed energy ...Perhaps, as Einstein believed, there is only a single energy, 'a unified field,' but if so it has countless faces. Numerous cultures describe a matrix of subtle energies that support, shape, and animate the physical body, called *qi* or *chi* in China, *prana* in the yoga tradition of India and Tibet, *yesod* in the Jewish cabalistic tradition, *ki* in Japan, *baraka* by the Sufis, *wakan* by the Lakotas, *orenda* by the Iriquois, *megbe* by the Ituri Pygmies, and the *Holy Spirit* in the Christian tradition.[1]

She looks back at ancient cultures and relates their concepts of a divine energy or energetic source to the modern Einsteinian theory of quantum physics.

Auras/Kirlian photo

Beyond the conjectures made from Einstein's theory, some practitioners will offer visual evidence to illustrate their claim. During the second half of the twentieth century a technological innovation came with the development of a photographic process called Kirlian photography. A high-voltage, high-frequency electronic photograph can be taken of a plant, human being or other living creature. When the photo print is developed it shows coloured flares of energy radiating around a plant's leaves, or the body of living creatures. There are scientific and mystical interpretations of Kirlian photography.

Both of us have had Kirlian photographs taken for the purposes of entering into further spiritual conversations. The psychic reader explained to us that the image that is reproduced on the photo is a visual image of what in older times would be called 'the halo'. She then discussed the meaning of our individual photos. One of us had white and orange lights around the ears with a stream of purple rising above the crown. The psychic remarked, 'The white and orange shows you are receiving true wisdom and sharing it with compassion.' The purple is the direct channel into the highest realm. The other photo was ablaze with red light, to which the psychic said, 'You are highly spiritually advanced.' The psychic then had an interesting moment when we said that we were Christians and were running a nearby exhibitor's booth!

The photograph clearly shows that there is a field of energy around us; the question is 'what is it?' One natural explanation is that this field is simply generated from body heat, and the conversion of its wave-lengths that turn into a band of colours. Another claim is that the energy photographed simply reflects the changing chemistry of the skin like heat and sweat. Others insist that it has nothing to do with our bodies but is the discharge of gas in the air.

The interpretation of the new spirituality practitioner is that the energy which is caught on the photo reveals a more mystical and spiritual side to all living matter in the universe. There is a universal life force that animates everything and it is the ultimate form of reality. Ultimate reality is normally described as 'all is one' and 'all is God'. What practitioners mean by the term 'God' is that there is a divine but impersonal energy or force. Nikki Goldstein an aromatherapist explains:

> My concept of Lifeforce is similar to both Prana and Qi, in that all three could be said to be energy, but I take Lifeforce to mean something more ... in almost every instance you could substitute the word Lifeforce for the words spirit, health, vitality, bliss, balance, joy, consciousness, illumination and love. Lifeforce is the force for good within us ... we evolve because the Lifeforce that flows through

our individual systems is literally programmed to seek out, and eventually merge with, its universal source ... the Lifeforce in all beings longs to unite with its universal creator.[2]

Reiki

One energy system of healing that originates from Japan is called Reiki. The discoverer of Reiki was Mikao Usui (1865-1925) who studied Christianity at Kyoto University and then did further study at a seminary in Chicago. He wanted to know how Jesus had healed people and did not find satisfactory answers. He then turned to Tibetan Buddhist sources and during a twenty-one day retreat, he believed he had discovered there is a universal life force or energy that can be accessed to heal others.

It is claimed by some followers of Usui that when he visited the Himalayas he found scrolls about Jesus having lived in Tibet and other parts of East Asia.[3] Jesus, it is claimed, studied Buddhist teaching, and this was hidden wisdom that he shared secretly with his closest disciples. During Usui's lifetime there were other Japanese teachers who claimed that there was evidence for Jesus having lived in Japan. There is no historical or biblical evidence to support these claims about Jesus being in Tibet or Japan.[4]

Reiki is often described by practitioners and users as a gentle, peaceful, form of healing where energy flows from the hands into the body. Reiki teachers refer to five principles that form the basis for being a healer:

- Just for today I will give thanks for my many blessings.
- Just for today I will not worry.
- Just for today I will not be angry.
- Just for today I will do my work honestly.
- Just for today I will be kind to my neighbour and every living thing.[5]

The Reiki method covers three areas for therapy, namely the head, front chest and back. The practitioner will either lay hands on these parts of the body or hover the hands just above. For particular ailments, including emotional and mental problems, the hands may be placed on the body where the illness is felt the worst. Reiki healers may use other healing tools, such as crystals, as part of therapy. The process of diagnosis involves an intuition that when energy is strongly transferred into the patient's body that is where the illness or concern is centred. The flow of energy may vary as the patient draws on what is channelled. Many healers explain that this transfer of energy is related to the existence of the chakras in our body. We discussed chakras in the previous chapter. Paula Horan gives this basic sketch:

> Reiki is never sent, it is drawn through the channel ... The energy enters at my crown chakra and passes through the upper energy centers to my heart and solar plexus. The rest then passes through my arms and hands to your body. I am thus never drained in the process, as a certain amount of energy is stored in me.[6]

When a student is trained in the technique of Reiki healing it is possible to engage in self-treatment.[7] Reiki healing may also be applied over long distances by transmitting energy to a person who is far away and in need. Reiki is not limited to healing people but is also used by some practitioners in healing pets.

Catherine Garrett is a sociologist who was searching for healing of chronic physical pain, and in that journey sampled Reiki. She chronicled her experiences as part of an academy study on alternate spiritual healing techniques. She observed:

> The language used depends to some extent on the particular Reiki Master (mine used a lot of New Age terms taken from her experience of other kinds of healing), but the story and the teaching of Reiki techniques was simple and jargon-free. Reiki deals with embodied people: it recognizes the inseparability of body, mind, and self ... it is taught as a means of healing the whole person, without making much distinction between physical and psychological suffering.[8]

Those who endorse Reiki generally insist that it is religiously neutral and can be adapted to any faith tradition. So you will encounter professing Catholics, born-again evangelicals, and Pentecostals who say there is 'Christian' Reiki. Reiki flourishes worldwide, and if you do a Google search there are many websites in different nations.

Reflexology
Reflexology is a bodywork therapy where massage is applied to the feet to promote health. It is claimed the soles of the feet are a map to our internal organs. By massaging specific points, energy is realised and a particular organ is treated.

Therapeutic Touch
Therapeutic Touch is a non-contact method of healing that was developed by the American nurse Dolores Krieger. Therapists attune themselves to patients by passing their hands across the body, but without physical touch. Once a problem has been identified by the hand sensing it, the therapist places a hand just above and channels an energy called prana into the patient. This process is meant to activate the patient's energy centres (or chakras) to heal. This is a method that is used by health care professionals in retirement villages, health centres and even in hospital wards.

Acupuncture/Acupressure
A friend of ours is a surgeon who for his professional work has travelled frequently to China. He found it interesting that while the west was exploring acupuncture, in China's medical facilities there was great interest in western methods of treatment. Acupuncture is rooted in ancient mystical Chinese belief of Chi, which is positive energy that flows through the human body. Illnesses arise when the flow of energy is not balanced. The remedy involves inserting needles at key pressure points (called meridians) to interrupt the flow of 'negative' energy and to allow the Chi to be harmonized. The needles trigger signals where the pain is located in the nervous system.

Acupressure is a variant approach where, instead of needles, fingers or hands are used on the pressure points to achieve the same outcomes. A Japanese version of acupressure is called Shiatsu.

There are different understandings of what happens when the body's pressure points are touched. Some practitioners do believe in the mystical Chinese concept of Chi but others simply state that the reason why acupuncture/acupressure 'works' is because the body is interconnected.

Crystals

Crystals such as quartz, emeralds and topaz are often on display in shopping malls, and sold both for jewellery and for good luck. Crystals are primarily used in the context of complementary healing as a conductor of energy to assist in healing. An old favourite is sapphire which is used to treat ulcers. Crystals may be placed on the body's chakras to generate the flow of energy. We have seen crystals used in a hospital ward where the stones were hung over a patient's bed, and when we asked our friend who put them there the surprising reply came, 'the doctor'.

Pantheism

The classic belief that 'all is one' and 'all is god' is an important concept for energy healers. Claims about a universal life force or universal energy dovetail in a pantheistic understanding of how the cosmos 'works'. Pantheism is expressed in some Hindu schools of thought and in ancient Chinese philosophy. Some ancient Greek philosophers taught it. Today there are pantheist currents found in some versions of alternate spiritualities in the west. It is a mistake to assume that everyone who explores alternate, 'New Age' spiritualities is pantheistic.[9]

Cultural change

In the introduction we observed that the west may be less Christian but remains very spiritual. The emergence of the global village has made it very easy to 'shop around' in all areas of life. The 'spiritual but not religious' and 'none' are accustomed to sampling a smorgasbord of tools and methods.

Another contributing element has been recently described by scholars as 'postsecular'. It used to be fashionable to claim that the western world had moved on from religious beliefs and was 'secular'. A theory that was popular among Marxists is that religion would vanish as scientific knowledge spread and as government institutions took over social roles once the domain of churches. The prediction that religion would vanish has proven false. The transfer of some social roles from churches to government or non-religious institutions has led to a 'secular' state. However, religious beliefs, whether in traditional bodies such as the church, or in new movements and alternate spiritualities, have not disappeared and some flourish.

> 'You are a spiritual being. You are energy, and energy cannot be recreated or destroyed—it just changes form. Therefore the pure essence of you has always been and always will be.'
>
> Rhonda Byrne, *The Secret* (New York, London, Toronto, Sydney: Atria Books, 2006), 175.

The 'postsecular' element is a basic recognition that religious beliefs persist and thrive. There is a strong yearning for authentic experiences beyond the material. The world never reached the goals predicted by secular theorists. Energy healing has emerged and continues to flourish as one facet of the 'postsecular'.

CONTACT POINTS

The growth of Pentecostal and Charismatic movements are clear indicators that people want a sense of hope, and to experience healing in their minds, bodies, and spirits. The yearnings for peace of mind, and for deep relief from physical and emotional pain, are all around us.

The contact points are global. Ross was in Nepal after the earthquake and the pastors and church leaders were crying out for practical help for themselves and their people. The question was raised whether we should go to energy healing and practices like yoga to give comfort and find relief. There was little western medicine available and the despair was widespread. Prayer was real and comforting but there was a sense of can't we do, give more. There was significant time spent talking about breathing, bodily postures, and emotional and physical healing.

In this 'age of healing' it is not uncommon to hear of a celebrity combining traditional medicine with energy healing. Their testimony impacts many.

DISCERNMENT

In the chapter on Hallowe'en we spoke of discerning spiritual forces. In the previous chapter we considered the role of the practitioner as a crucial consideration. Here we want to reiterate the importance and value of listening. Our investigation of energy healing has shown us that people trust what they feel and value their experiences. Linda Woodhead is a sociologist and theologian and has pointed out that not everyone is the same in the way they experience and know things. Some people are what she dubs a 'boundless self', meaning they are very open to exploring and sampling things. They do not sit well with ways of knowing that are limited to narrow categories. Experience, creativity, and self-expression are highly valued.

> 'The maxim 'understanding precedes criticism' must become the watch-word of all Christians who feel called to evangelize members of new religions.'
> Irving Hexham and Karla Poewe-Hexham, 'New Religions in Global Cultures' in *Encountering New Religious Movements*, Ed. Irving Hexham, Stephen Rost and John W. Morehead (Grand Rapids: Kregel, 2004), 111.

Many in the church are what she calls a 'bestowed self'. The emphasis is on a source of authority such as the Bible and pastor for discovering truth. For a 'boundless self' the starting point is not any external source of authority, rather it is 'does this work?' They are more likely to rely on personal experiences, the testimony of others, and trusting one's intuition before they turn to any authority.[10]

It is important to listen and hear a person's story before talking about 'errors' in beliefs. If we fail to do this, we are not only being discourteous, but we run the risk in conversation of being like two boats that pass each other.

Some years ago William Johnston, the Catholic theologian and expert on Zen, ran workshops on mysticism. He placed all his emphasis on coming to terms with the 'dark night of the soul'. A question was posed to him, but 'how do we find ways to live with chronic physical pain?' Johnston had to admit that this was not a question that he had reflected on. His experience of the spiritual had not led him to appreciate the problem of the physical body. He had missed a key element in the spiritual search of those attending. By listening we hear what the priorities of others are in a holistic sense rather than our simply centring on questions of heresy, or matters we want to concentrate on. Often we offer answers for questions that people are not asking. Those who explore energy healing are asking questions about emotional and physical well-being.

Nevertheless, we find that traditional practitioners of energy healing do hold to a worldview, and that may lead to important questions about differences in beliefs. In this area a big difference is either relying on God for healing and guidance, or we simply being part of an impersonal universalised energy. The opening page of the Bible is clear that God is not identical with the universe but is the personal creator. We are finite creatures, not God. This is driven home when Pagans saw Paul and Barnabas as gods. Paul made it clear, 'We also are men, of like nature with you, and we bring you good news, that you should turn from these vain things to a living God, who made

the heaven and the earth and the sea and all that is in them'
(Acts 14: 15-16). Obviously, from a Christian perspective,
healing is in a dependent relationship on God through prayer
and the ministry of the Holy Spirit.

In much western energy healing we are not reliant on a
personal Creator but are 'one' with a higher power. We control
life's script. Deepak Chopra, a major New Spirituality writer, has
recently responded to the New Atheism of Richard Dawkins in
The Future of God. Chopra represents the view of pantheism suited
for the west:

> You merge with your source. God is revealed as pure consciousness,
> the essence of who you are ... Your individual ego has expanded to
> become a cosmic ego ... In reality you are completely connected to
> God already.[11]

The contrasts are tabled below.

WESTERN PANTHEISM	CHRISTIAN
GOD	GOD
Monism (all is one) Pantheism (all is god)	Personal Creator (Genesis 1 & 2) Sovereign over creation
SELF	SELF
Divine/good Control our destiny	Creature is not divine, but made in the image of God (Gen. 1:26-28; Psalm 8)
JESUS	JESUS
The guru who for some travelled to India Christ Consciousness (salvation is discovering that we, like Jesus, are 'one' with the Father— partake in divinity) resurrection	Lord and God Salvation is in Christ not ourselves; grace; the cross and resurrection (John 20:28 & 1 Cor. 15: 3-5

CASE STUDIES

There are Christians who specialise in ministries of constructive critique who raise questions about energy healing. This is particularly evident in ministries that focus on pinpointing heresy, and conduct seminars for churches on discernment. This approach is represented by writers such as Elliot Miller of the Christian Research Institute who seek to positively equip the church to discern truth from heresy.[12] Others, whilst heeding those concerns, have developed models of neutral or 'Christian Reiki'. They are adamant that their sole guide is Jesus Christ and they do not advocate pantheism or contact with spirits. 'Reiki energy comes from God as expression of His unconditional love.'[13]

Energy healing we have found is very appropriate as a topic for preaching and bible studies. It touches on worldview and beliefs, healing and wholeness, and the search for meaning. People find it relevant and helpful.

We know of churches that are developing well-being centres that offer services in counselling and legal advice and the emphasis is on general well-being. Some are exploring medical assistance and potential use of complementary remedies. One example is Burrswood Church in England which is known for its healing centre where chaplains offer counselling, prayer and healing exercises (e.g. Ignatian meditative exercises) for those who stay in its small hospital.[14] In the United States the Home for Health Lifestyle Center provides residential stay facilities for people who are already receiving traditional medical treatment. The Center provides programmes to further assist well-being with prayer, counsel, vegetarian food, and some complementary methods of healing.[15]

Another well-being approach which is holistic but not directly related to energy healing, is the ministry centred programmes like 'Essence'. At the start of this century the evangelist Rob Frost and his team developed 'Essence,' and it still enjoys some use today in mission outreach. It is a practical tool that is worth revisiting.

'*Essence*' was devised with two broad things in mind. First, it is a resource tool that responds to the broad social hunger outside the church for some tangible spiritual practice. Second, it could also be used for personal enhancement in one's Christian spiritual growth.

'*Essence*' was created as a six-session course where a facilitator guided participants through themes such as our journey so far, journey within, toward a better world, wholeness, spirituality, the future. The sessions were experientially focused and made use of passages from scripture, postures, using our hands in prayer, tools like Labyrinths, group activities and reflections. One group activity in the session 'journeying to the future' involved participants selecting ribbons that reflected their level of optimism or pessimism and attaching the ribbon to a length of rope. The participants could then express their hopes and fears concerning the future. The facilitator then rounded the session up with an expression of Christian hope drawn from Revelation 22:1-5.[16] We believe that within this course it is possible for a time of reflection and practice of Christian healing to be included.

Local churches that conduct healing services as a missional outreach could consider exploring the issue of God's Spirit working throughout the creation as the ultimate source of energy healing. We have found in such services fruitful conversations unfold with people attracted to energy healing who have not come to an understanding of God as a personal creator. It is helpful in the service to explore the Old Testament's understanding of God's Spirit (Hebrew term: *ruach*) at work in the creation. The Old Testament's witness is that God's Spirit is actively giving life and sustaining it in all people and in all living creatures (Job 12:10; 27:3; Ps. 104:29-30; Gen. 2:7; 6:17). God's Spirit is the energetic source of all life in the sphere of creation.

We can expand on this understanding by considering how God's providential care is not restricted to followers of Jesus. God provides rain for the benefit of all people and all creatures (Matt. 5:45; Acts 14:17). The Bible gives examples of people who received divine healing but who did not necessarily repent and follow

Christ (Luke 17:12-17; cf. 2 Kings 5:1-14). God may at times respond in mercy and his healing may even flow from the hands of a practitioner of energy healing.

Conversations along these lines have also taken place in alternate spirituality festivals that we and others are part of. As we have mentioned such festivals or community 'markets' are not difficult for churches or para church groups to be part of. The wonderful opportunity is there to gently and respectfully challenge a pantheistic practitioner of energy healing to discover that the ultimate source for healing is the personal Creator through the Holy Spirit.[17]

THINGS TO DO

Consider the approach of this church. One Sunday morning, instead of the sermon, the congregation was encouraged to leave the building and to investigate what people were doing that morning who do not attend church. They were encouraged to enter into conversations with people to discover what they were interested in and why they did not visit the church. A small survey could be completed on their view of the local church. This allowed the church to consider in what way it was not making holistic connections to the local community. The members of the congregation shared their experiences the following Sunday. What they discovered was an organic market which included exhibitors providing alternate healing services, while others were in a park practicing yoga. On basis of the feedback we were asked as consultants to help shape ministry direction.

START THE CONVERSATION

1. 'The role of God's Spirit in the creation includes providential acts of healing for people outside the church.' Discuss this in light of your understanding of the Bible and energy healing.

2. In your group talk about what therapies you would explore for healing and well-being.
3. With your non-Christian friends ask what role prayer would play in their life in a time of sickness or distress. How do they view alternative therapies?
4. Why are people in the West today drawn to alternative healing processes outside of traditional medicine?

5
MEDITATION (MINDFULNESS, TM) –
Coping tool or religion?

We hear from concerned Christians that churches appear to have been caught unaware of the sudden popular upsurge in the practice of 'eastern' meditation.[1] It is touted to be the unifying religious practice, and it is manifested in Mindfulness Meditation and Transcendental Meditation (TM) in particular.

'It would not be an exaggeration to say that in the last decade the approach which has dominated counselling in the Western world is what has been called 'mindfulness' ... many helpful outcomes have been described from its use, varying from peace of mind for anyone, to release from chronic depression and addictions for some.'

Bill Andersen, *Walking alongside: a theology for people-helpers* (Eugene, Oregon: Wipf & Stock, 2013), 157.

Mindfulness is praised as the way forward for handling life better. 'Life is difficult' are the opening words of Scott Peck's *The Road Less Travelled*, which in the 1980s gave birth to the self-help movement. How to handle the ache of life, what is it that 'bugs you,' is *the* issue that many people really want to handle. Mindfulness is advertised with no religious content and invites experiences of personal transformation. We become peaceful, compassionate and non-judgmental. As a discipline it is adaptable to Buddhist, Christian and Secular settings.

The Guardian gives us a taste of what it is like:

> In a first floor room above a gridlocked London street, 20 strangers shuffle on to mats and cushions. There's an advertising executive, a personnel manager, a student and a pensioner. A gong sounds softly and a session of meditation begins. This is one of more than 1,000 mindfulness courses proliferating across the UK as more and more people struggling with anxiety, depression and stress turn towards a practice adapted from a 2,400-year-old Buddhist tradition.

The paper goes on to say that, 'Mindfulness is spreading fast into village halls, schools and hospitals and even the offices of banks and internet giants such as Google.'[2] Melanie McDonagh wryly observes, 'It seems to be the perfect religion for a Britain which is in full flight from its state church.'[3] Such flourishing reports are true of the West as a whole. America was the cauldron from which mindfulness meditation was popularised and adapted by professor of medicine Jon Kabat-Zinn. In Australia one of our favourite football teams, the South Sydney Rabbitohs, uses it as part of their winning strategy.

Mindfulness is so extensive in its influence that it is under the scrutiny of educationalists. Significant universities, such as Oxford and Brown, are undertaking major research projects into the benefits, and medical and psychological drawbacks of Mindfulness. We will discuss the benefits and drawbacks in our discernment section. Public schools are conducting trials and suggesting it has 'overwhelming benefits' in helping to defuse stress. 'It's all about thinking about students focus, breathing, getting in and just being centred before they start their day of academic work.'[4] In the US its efficacy is being carefully studied in the public school system.[5]

TM is a grass-roots movement which had a presence that is similar to that of Mindfulness. It appeared to go into decline in the 1990s but it is having a rebirth. Its initial popularity came with The Beatles in the 1960s and today enjoys celebrity endorsements including media mogul Rupert Murdoch, Hollywood director David Lynch and CNN anchor Candy Crowley.[6]

Deepak Chopra, the Indian-born American-based new spirituality teacher and author, began his spiritual discipline in TM. His approach has broadened from those roots. His Chopra Centre recommends the benefits of meditation for improving health and well-being. The approach he takes is very practical and typifies the way in which many people make use of meditation as part of their daily routine. One dedicates a space at home or in an office or outdoor setting for meditation and then a mood for meditation may be invoked by lighting a candle to gaze at. The meditative technique uses the same set of breathing exercises found in Hatha Yoga, which we explained in chapter one. Besides the breathing exercises, a practitioner is encouraged to sit or lie still and, by using visualisation, becomes aware of different parts of the body going into a state of relaxation. The technique also includes singing or chanting a mantra. Bess O'Connor of the Chopra Centre recommends exciting children's interest in chanting a mantra:

> OM is the sound of the universe and divine intelligence: kids can connect with that! The sound can range from a strange harmonious choir to the sound of different animals howling in the jungle.[7]

BACKGROUND

TM

The story of TM in the West begins with the Indian-born guru Maharishi Mahesh Yogi (1918-2008). He graduated from the University of Allahabad in 1942 with a degree in physics. He then became a disciple of Swami Brahmananda Saraswati (1869-1953), also known as Guru Dev, who was the head of a prominent Hindu monastery. For twelve years the Maharishi studied the Hindu text, known as the Bhagavad-Gita, and the practice of Transcendental

Meditation which uses a mantra. TM is centred in two main things: sacred devotion to the guru and realising one's inner divinity through chanting a mantra in meditation. In TM one discovers that we are one with the divine (pantheism):

> The individual in all his various aspects of life is the light of God, the impersonal absolute Being ... Without divine consciousness, man is found lacking in energy, intelligence, and clear thinking. He is tired, worried, tense and anxious.[8]

In 1959 the Maharishi relocated from India to Los Angeles where he established the Spiritual Regeneration Movement as the vehicle for teaching TM. He reorganised the movement in 1965 and changed its name to the Students International Meditation Society. It was at this time of reorganisation that Maharishi's TM became renowned because celebrities, including the Beatles and Beach Boys, studied it. Many youth followed their example and practiced TM in the 1960s and 1970s. At that time the Church concentrated its attention on philosophical academic debates and missed the direction being taken by the person on the street. John Drane declared in a sermon:

> All this is just another way of saying that the Gospel needs to be people-centred and not predominately idea-centred. We need to listen to what ordinary people are saying, and recognize that in many ways it is not the same as the ideologies of intellectual post-modernity ... I often wonder where we might be today if, instead of listening to the voices of those few theologians who spoke of 'the death of God' back then, we had paid more attention to the icons of popular culture – people like the Beatles, who never had any problem at all with transcendence, but inspired a whole generation to head off in new directions to search for spiritual meaning in some unexpected places.[9]

TM is relatively simple to practice. It requires one to meditate for twenty minutes in the morning and the same at night. One sits cross-legged in the lotus position and meditates quietly repeating a single word mantra: a divine word or divine name. During the 1970s in the USA some teachers of TM tried to introduce it into public schools. In 1977 there was a civil action taken in New Jersey by concerned parents. They argued that as TM was Hindu it could not be taught in public schools because it was a breach of the US constitution on the separation of church and state. The court weighed up the evidence presented about the Maharishi's teachings and the religious purpose of the mantra. The initiation ceremony into TM involved a Sanskrit chant where the initiate bowed down to 'the galaxy of the gods'. The court's verdict was that TM was indeed Hindu and that it could not be taught in public schools.[10]

Mindfulness Meditation

'I think the benefit of mindfulness is something that most of the big institutions in the City now recognise and support. Employers increasingly understand that they can only really maximise the full potential of their employees if they are well functioning, healthy and resilient. Employers have been encouraging physical fitness among employees for some time now with gym memberships – supporting mindfulness is the next step. It makes sense from a business perspective.'

Eva Luterkort, in 'Mindfulness meditation is big business in London's Square Mile,' *The Independent*, 14 March 2015.

Recently, Philip's wife Ruth was obliged in her capacity as a legal manager in a government department to attend a two-day management seminar. The seminar was Mindful Leadership Global Forum. Some four hundred leaders from over two hundred companies and government departments were in attendance. The speakers included Australian sports icon Paul Roos (Melbourne Football Club) and corporate executives from firms like IBM. The theme was productivity, performance and purpose. The focus was on controlling stress, improving staff productivity and cultivating compassion. The way to realise these outcomes is Mindfulness Meditation, which was touted as a 'robustly secular' way for achieving serenity.

Some Mindfulness ideas that the speakers presented include breath control, discovering those thoughts that trigger or coincide with stress and learning how to become detached from stressful thoughts. The seminar popularised some meditative techniques that Dr Kabat-Zinn developed in his psychotherapeutic approach called Mindfulness Meditation Stress Reduction (MMSR). Kabat-Zinn devised MMSR after he had made a prolonged study of both Zen and Vipassana Buddhism. He borrowed both the concept of 'mindfulness' and the meditative breathing technique from Vipassana Buddhism. Vipassana Buddhism is a particular school of thought, sometimes also called Insight Meditation, which flourishes in India, Burma and Thailand.[11] Although Kabat-Zinn says that he is not a Buddhist, his therapeutic MMSR draws its inspiration from Vipassana. Kabat-Zinn explains:

> Mindfulness is an ancient Buddhist practice which has profound relevance for our present-day lives. This relevance has nothing to do with Buddhism per se or with becoming a Buddhist, but it has everything to do with waking up and living in harmony with oneself and with the world. It has to do with examining who we are, with questioning our view of the world and our place in it, and with cultivating some appreciation for the fullness of each moment we are alive. Most of all, it has to do with being in touch.[12]

Kabat-Zinn spearheaded the creation of Mindfulness as a therapeutic tool which is now widely used in the field of counselling. Mindfulness has also been modified by people who have a clear interest in meditation as a spiritual tool. Many Mindfulness programmes or workshops have been devised for popular consumption; including Buddhist, others are Christian, and there are those that are secular.

MEDITATION

At the seminar Ruth attended, there was no overt commitment to Vipassana nor was the seminar devised to indoctrinate people. However, both the meditative breathing technique and the message to cultivate compassion, reflected the tenets of Vipassana. Most speakers approached Mindfulness as a helpful tool for dealing with inner stress-related thoughts. Reactions in the audience were mixed as some were excited, others circumspect and a couple of tough-minded atheists were unimpressed. Ruth noted though that the tone of some speakers' testimonies reminded her of revival meetings.

In general Mindfulness Meditation sessions involve guiding the practitioner in exercises of awareness of the body, breathing and surroundings. The goal of the meditation is to achieve stillness and calm, to view people and everything else through the eyes of compassion and non-judgment.

In a common therapeutic approach, known as Acceptance and Commitment Therapy (ACT), Mindfulness consists of six core processes. It is worth noting that these same points are also found in many popular Mindfulness programmes:

1. **Connection**: means being in the present moment; connecting with what's going on here and now.
2. **Defusion**: means to step back, or to detach, from worrying thoughts and memories. Instead of being swept up by your thoughts, or trying to dump them, one learns to let them pass by. It is just like looking out the window and seeing the traffic come and go. Here is an exercise in how it is done: I am having a negative thought such as 'I am incompetent'. I now insert in front of this phrase the words, 'I am having the thought that ...'. It is suggested that, when one runs the negative thought again with the new phrase in front of it, there is a distance from the thought, and it has much less impact. There has been no effort to get rid of the thought, nor to change it. Instead the relationship with the thought has changed. It can be seen as just words.
3. **Expansion** (acceptance): means opening up to painful feelings without being overwhelmed by them.

4. **Observing Self**: understanding the part of your mind that is able to be aware of whatever it is that you are thinking.
5. **Values**: what you want to stand for and what matters the most to you.
6. **Committed Action**: doing it.[13]

Mindfulness is undergoing rigorous testing and there is significant frontier research on it benefits. Scott and Melissa Symington are Fuller Theological Seminary graduates with doctorates in clinical psychology. In their peer-reviewed paper they itemise the following applications of Mindfulness in treating problems such as depression, anxiety, compulsive behaviours, life transitions, relational difficulties, and sexual dysfunction.[14] Many counsellors and health-care professionals believe that Mindfulness is a great tool for helping people with depression. A study conducted at Johns Hopkins University School of Medicine has noted that mindfulness programmes may help reduce anxiety, depression and stress. The efficacy of meditation for reducing blood-pressure is widely acknowledged.

In Sydney, the helpline counselling service, Lifeline, has noted that 2015 was a record year as they had one million phone calls. Lifeline indicated that problems with depression were extensive among their callers and that problems of loneliness and isolation seem to be exacerbated by the excessive use of new mobile digital communications devices.

CONTACT POINTS

The prevalence of the disciplines of Mindfulness meditation is almost ubiquitous in the community. It is in corporate settings, education, counselling, psychology, self-help books, sports, and festivals. TM, and other meditative disciplines, are found in many of the same settings. Meditation in Christian circles may be found in congregations, monasteries and convents.

DISCERNMENT

Christian meditation is biblically valid and has played a significant part in the emergence of spiritual disciplines in church history. We will touch on the question of Christian approaches to meditation later in the chapter. With respect to Mindfulness and TM there are important matters for discernment which we need to sift through. Christian responses to Mindfulness and TM tend to follow the same pattern of responses to the topics such as yoga and energy healing: there are those who reject it; there are those who take it as it is; others who seek to redeem it and Christianise. No matter which of the responses that resonates the most for you, we all need to take the time to discern and reflect.

Perhaps the best starting point is to consider what kind of Mindfulness Meditation programme you may encounter. There are some programmes that are explicitly Buddhist, not just in their origins, but also in the direction that they take. If we encounter a Mindfulness meditation class or workshop that openly declares it is 'Vipassana' mediation, then we are definitely looking at a group that is committed to a particular understanding of Buddhist faith. Key figures who represent Vipassana or Insight Meditation include Jack Kornfield, S. N. Goenka, and William Hart.

In general there are several critical points for discernment that various commentators have expressed about Mindfulness in considering whether it or its offshoots, is 'taboo or to do?' We have condensed their concerns and sorted them into four critical points.

Respect

Part of the Christian walk entails respecting the position of non-Christian practitioners which is at the heart of Peter's advice that in giving reasons for faith we do so with gentleness and respect (1 Pet. 3:15). There are deeply committed Buddhists who are disturbed at the way in which Mindfulness has been disconnected from the way of the Buddha and reshaped into programmes that concentrate on therapeutic relief. The Buddhist alarm is similar to what we saw in our yoga chapter, where some traditional Hindus believe that westerners disrespect and 'dumb-down' yoga.

If we are in a missional paradigm we need to exercise great care when using a given discipline. We need to manifest integrity and be honest about what we are doing. We run the risk at times of being hurtful rather than being effective in missional terms.

Social Justice and Individualism

Ronald Purser is a committed Buddhist who offers very perceptive criticism of the popular adaptations of Mindfulness. One major point he makes is that Mindfulness programmes used in corporate settings operate with a highly privatised view of self that is divorced from the public sphere. Most of these programmes limit the source of stress to the individual's internal private life, and the remedy offered is to rectify the personal problem. What is critically excluded from analysis is that organisational systems contribute a lot to the experience of stress and anger. The implication is that the individual is to blame for their problem and Mindfulness is shaped as a tool that intervenes at the private personal level. The corporation's structures get off scot-free from being exposed to evaluation.

Another important point Purser discusses concerns the absence of a social ethic inside the corporation. A Mindfulness programme may tantalise employees with a taste of feeling temporary relief, while sustaining a work environment that is unrelenting in exhausting and sapping the strength of employees. Purser exhorts 'corporate mindfulness programs have succeeded in creating ... privatized glimpses of stress reduction and enhanced focussed attention while mindlessly externalizing macro-tensions and structural inequalities'.[15] Simultaneously the programme may divert customer attention away from calling the corporation's activities into question on controversial matters like company tax-evasion, and violations of a customer's privacy.

MEDITATION

Earlier in the chapter we spoke of Ruth's experience at a seminar. It was apparent to her that some participants could see the disparity between the promises of personal stress reduction while leaving the stressful status quo of the corporation's structures unchanged. In our missional and life journey with Jesus many of us will apply the Micah 6:8 test, 'and what does the Lord require of you but to do justice, and to love kindness, and to walk humbly with your God'.

The other concern is that many Mindfulness programmes cater to a high-sense of individualism that is divorced from any sense of community. In a Trinitarian understanding of spirituality a Christian appreciates that God is both one and many. The three centres of personhood, the Father, Son and Spirit, form a community for relationships. As Christians we honour the individual but always seeing the individual as belonging in relationship to the community. Jesus' high priestly prayer teaches us that we should be one just as the Father and Son are one (John 17:21). The Apostle Paul reminds us that our gifts for ministry are meant for the common good (1 Cor. 12:4-7).

Purser speaks as a Buddhist in flamboyant terms concerning North American culture but there is embedded in his colourful rhetoric some truism we all would want to keep in mind:

'Depression, anxiety, and myriad other forms of human suffering present themselves as problems to be solved in much the same way as getting the car repaired, cleaning a dirty floor, or balancing the check-book. Humans are problem solvers. Wherever we go we find problems to solve. As therapists, we are often swept up, without questioning, in the client's problem-solving agenda.'

Kelly G. Wilson and Emily K. Sandoz, 'Mindfulness, Values and Therapeutic Relationship in Acceptance and Commitment Therapy', in *Mindfulness and the Therapeutic Relationship*, S. Hick and T. Bein Eds (New York: Guildford, 2008), 91.

North Americans' self-concept is one of a highly individualistic and atomized unit in society, with little commitment to community or tradition ... This cultural bias places a heavy burden on the individual, as the source of suffering is viewed as a lack of self-regulation and entirely self-made. Mindfulness-based interventions are in close resonance with the ideological basis for 'blaming the victim,' as it is the individual (not the social context, history, or facts such as socio-economic status, inequities) that is held fully responsible for their own emotional reactivity, mental suffering and misery, as well as their own illnesses.[16]

Holistic

Another area for critical reflection concerns the limits of Mindfulness programmes, in particular the extent to which there are gaps in it being truly holistic. Daniel Siegel is a pioneer in neuroscience as it relates to the study of Mindfulness.[17] He is also personally committed to the Buddhist way of life. Siegel insists that Mindfulness provides the key to remedying our problems. By turning inward we have access to truth and our inner awareness of our thoughts will enable us to take control of our problems. His neuroscientific research is warmly regarded by various commentators for showing a deep connection between our inward state and the practical benefits of Mindfulness.

It is also worth noting that other scientists, such as Andrew Newberg, have been studying neuroscience and genetics and their positive connections to spirituality. Newberg's observations about how we are hardwired in our brains and genes for spirituality lead him to the understanding that for spiritual stories to be truly transformative they must become spiritual experiences. Rituals and disciplines like meditation give us, Newberg says, a 'good taste of God'. Christian journals have taken note of Newberg's research, and affirmed that meditation, prayer and faith are good for the psychological functioning of the brain.[18]

Two people we greatly respect in areas of spirituality and discernment are Bill Andersen and John Drane. Bill is a theologian, who held worldwide leadership roles in Scripture

Union. Both have been quite positive about the frontier research findings of neuroscience and spirituality. They have, however, also raised certain questions we need to consider. Bill Andersen raises a valid concern about the beneficial results that come when we turn inward. In particular, he questions Siegel's view that when we go inwards, and monitor our thoughts, we will become our own best friend. Here Siegel assumes that we will always treat ourselves well however this is not always the case: We are not always our own best friend. Andersen is not persuaded that we have an unsullied inborn capacity to make truthful self-assessments. He remarks that we do not always look after ourselves and we face a struggle under our own steam to become compassionate toward others. He argues that, in Siegel's approach to Mindfulness, God is left out of the picture and the endpoint is a very humanist outlook. Siegel's model gives no room for classic Christian teaching about the fall, grace, redemption and transforming power of the Holy Spirit.

The other concern, which John Drane raises, is that some forms of spirituality, such as for the reasons just noted, may be harmful, and so one must exercise discernment. Andersen sums up a critical Christian reservation about Siegel's Mindfulness:

> The biblical approach denies the possibility of generating one's own unsullied capabilities, and therefore relies upon a loving and searching God, to display his good news and, where there is genuine response, to begin his work of character transformation individually and corporately. Relationship with God, for the Christian, is primary, and leads toward relationship with others and also with ourselves.[19]

Worldview

The first point to keep in focus is that Buddhist understandings of reality take a significantly different direction to those in Christianity. Buddhist views of God and self, and the path to finding transformation and release from suffering, are markedly different from the Christian understanding of God, self, transformation, and suffering. For Buddhists, there is either no God at all or deities are unimportant in the final scheme of things. Buddhist enlightenment shows us that self is ultimately an illusory thing. It denies the notion of 'I', the soul and spirit. Vietnamese Buddhist teacher, Thich Nhat Hanh, who is widely known in the west as a respected practitioner of meditation, describes the Buddhist way as a fruit that you may like to try:

> Buddhism is more of a way of life than a religion. It is like a fruit. You may like a number of fruits, like bananas, oranges, mandarins, and so on. You are committed to eating these fruits. But then someone tells you that there is a fruit called mango and it would be wonderful for you to try that fruit. It will be a pity if you don't know what a mango is. But eating a mango does not require you to abandon your habit of eating oranges. Why not try it? You may like it a lot. Buddhism is a kind of mango, you see – a way of life, an experience that is worth trying. It is open for everyone.[20]

Christianity takes a different route: God is personal and is our creator to whom we are accountable. He is not just one of the options. The 'I' does exist as humans are made in God's image and likeness. Our spiritual problem is rooted in sin which is rebellion against God and others and the pathway to transformation of self and community is in relationship to the power of the risen Jesus Christ as our Lord and Saviour.[21]

Another point is that the secular approach to Mindfulness leaves God out of the picture, and shares in all the same weaknesses that Andersen and Drane referred to.

It is also wise to be alert to faddish elements that have become attached to Mindfulness. In 2015 the use of colouring-in-books in conjunction with Mindfulness was being praised as the latest exciting trend. There is no doubt that taking time out to de-stress in an activity such as colouring-in-books may have benefits. However, no sooner had 2016 dawned than the 'latest' trend is to apply the Japanese art of paper-folding known as origami with Mindfulness exercises. According to the ever shifting pop cultural trends for Mindfulness, colouring-in-books are 'out' and origami is now 'in'.

Christian Approach to Mindfulness

We know Christians who, operating under the Incarnational model we discussed in the Introduction, are using the therapeutic approach to Mindfulness, or the more popular workplace model. They are not only well aware of the above concerns but also have taken those concerns on board in what they do. Scott and Melissa Symington, the clinical psychologists whom we mentioned above, give us this helpful reminder that 'Christians are free to extract and employ a truthful principle while not embracing the religious or philosophical tradition to which it is attached'.[22] John Calvin expressed the same thought this way:

> If we regard the Spirit of God as the sole fountain of truth, we shall neither reject the truth itself, nor despise it wherever it shall appear, unless we wish to dishonour the Spirit of God ... If the Lord has willed that we be helped in physics, dialectic, mathematics, and other like disciplines, by the work and ministry of the ungodly, let us use this assistance.[23]

Several commentators agree with the view expressed by the Symingtons that there are three important pillars that are integral to a Christian approach to mindfulness. The first is presence of mind. The Bible upholds the importance of the place of the mind and that it must be renewed (Rom. 12:2). Paul exhorted that 'whatever is honourable, whatever is just, whatever is pure, whatever is lovely, whatever is commendable, if there is any excellence, if there is anything worthy of praise, think about these things' (Phil. 4:8).

A gospel narrative that is often used to illustrate the importance of a focused mind is the account of Peter walking on water (Matt. 14:22-33). It 'illustrates the need for mindfulness and the importance of focusing on the front screen (Jesus)'. Peter steps out of the boat with great faith but then allows his side-screen, filled with anxious images, to take hold. He saw the wind and waves and was sunk by fear. Feelings of fear are unavoidable but disaster happened when he focused on the side-screen rather than the front screen.

The second pillar is acceptance. We need to learn to let go of unwanted thoughts and feelings whilst accepting the threats and pains of life. The lesson is about not spending large amounts of time trying to manage thoughts and feelings that are beyond our control. Jesus calls us not to be anxious (Matt. 6:25-34).

The third pillar is internal observation. We know what it is like to be hurt by innuendo and unwarranted criticism. However, when one reaches a stage where one understands what the game is being played against them, and can become an observer of the game rather than the ball, they are empowered. It is about observing the feeling rather than being the feeling. At times we have to find a healthy detachment. Ambrose Ih-Ren Mong says:

> Internal observation suggests that the person learns to be detached from his feelings and thus becomes less reactionary. Feeling detached, he can say, 'I have this feeling of anxiety' instead of saying, 'I am anxious'. He does not let his anxiety control or define him.[24]

TM

The critical point of discernment is that TM is integrally a Hindu path. The mantra that initiates are given by their instructor draws one into a devotional practice with a Hindu deity. The mantra is meant to bring one into an experience of unity with the divine. The goal of TM is not just achieving temporary stress reduction but is about entering into a relationship with Hindu deities. For the seriously committed practitioner, one may also take additional instruction to acquire paranormal powers, known as siddhis, which may include an ability to 'levitate' (the capacity to launch your body in the lotus position up into the air repeatedly).

Advocates of the heresy and spiritual warfare models that we spoke about in the Introduction have raised the issue of discernment about the Hindu orientation of TM. They have also drawn attention to the personal concerns expressed by former TM teachers:

> As I got deeper into TM, I lost all desire for personal prayer and Bible reading. My concept of God as a Person and of Jesus Christ as mediator ... gradually changed during the years I was involved with TM to accommodate the Hindu concept of God as impersonal.[25]

Christian Meditation

Christian meditation and the contemplative disciplines are rooted in biblical thought, and well known for their expression in the early Desert Fathers, monastic traditions, and writers like Thomas á Kempis *The Imitation of Christ*, and Ignatius Loyola's spiritual exercises.[26] In contemporary spiritual writings we have a broad church such as Richard Foster, John Piper, and Dallas Willard.

In our journey we have been indebted to Lynda Rose who is a former TM teacher and now an Anglican. No matter where one stands in regards to the above, she sees great value in meditation for the Christian way of life and witness. Together with good breathing and posture, we have distilled four insights from her approach to Christian meditation:

- First: prepare yourself by finding a quiet spot and identifying your purpose for meditation.
- Second: choose one or more of the following God-centring aids for focus. A passage of Scripture; a word like 'peace,' 'Jesus' or 'love'; the Eastern Orthodox Jesus Prayer ('Lord Jesus Christ, Son of God, have mercy on me'); silence (that is, being still to allow God to talk to you: he leads the soul to pray); creation (seeing the handiwork of God).
- Third: conclude your exercise. 'The ending of meditation should be the same. It should be relaxed and end with a brief prayer of thanks and dedication, and the eyes should only then be opened, slowly.'[27]

105

- Fourth: be prepared for distractions such as pain, headaches, and drifting into sleep. Acknowledge them, do not be deterred, gently refocus your attention on the exercise and, the more experienced you become, the less these things will occur.

CASE STUDIES

Christian meditation also opens up missional horizons for local gatherings in all kinds of settings, which may include a church hall, or a spirituality festival. Examples for inspiration may be found in the writings of those we mentioned above such as the Desert Fathers.

For those who are interested in a missional connection, we have found the Lynda Rose approach to be amenable in seminars in numerous environments. There are also the examples to refer back to in our chapter on Yoga, where we described the approach of PraiseMoves, Holy Yoga, and Bede Griffiths.

A holistic spirituality model for the church and community has been developed by the Revd Guy Yeomans, a former member of the New South Wales Parliament who later trained as a Baptist minister. He did post-graduate work on mediation. Over the ten years he has been a pastor, his small local suburban church grew from an average attendance of about 22 to over 70. Of this increase about one third joined the church through the emphasis on meditation and, as he has indicated, some are from a Catholic background, others lapsed Protestants who had been 'burnt or dried out' and some eliciting a new spiritual awareness or hunger. In a recent survey of his congregation about half nominated the emphasis on spirituality as one of the top three reasons why they joined or have remained in the church. Once a month he offers a monthly one-hour meditation in the Christian tradition.

The group provides an opportunity for people to participate in meditation. Attendees are provided a handout which explains the historical background to Christian meditation, some biblical basis, techniques that are similar between Christian and Eastern meditation, and the following tips which are also reproduced on the church's website:

- A quiet unhurried atmosphere
- A relaxed mind and body
- Good posture (lying flat on your back; kneeling or sitting straight but not stiff back)
- Focus on breathing – long, slow deep breaths from the diaphragm
- Pray a 'prayer of the heart' – slowly, deliberately and repeatedly; e.g. 'Lord have mercy', or the Lord's prayer, reciting each word in time with your breathing
- Discipline. Set aside time regularly. Start modestly.
- Perseverance to keep returning to God and the meditative focus when distractions come.
- Meditate on Scripture, especially the gospel stories. Imagine being in the scene, engaging all the senses. Then let the Holy Spirit guides what happens.
- A sense of poverty and humility.
- A hunger and thirst for the things of God.
- Rely on the Holy Spirit. He is God on our side, our ultimate helper.[28]

The church service style includes periods of silence, use of liturgies, candles, banners and artworks, more reflective style of contemporary music, as well as traditional hymns. The ministry includes an annual retreat which provides sustained opportunity to practise the above meditation exercises. People are also encouraged to undertake private silent retreats and to avail themselves of other retreats that may be available. This spirituality emphasis is evident in the preaching and pastoral care of the church.

At a therapeutic level there are several Christian practitioners we have referred to in this chapter. The Symingtons in California as mentioned give one approach. In Australia, Anglican minister, the Revd Brett Morgan, conducts his practice in Acceptance and Commitment Therapy. He concentrates on the active types referred to above, e.g. connection, defusion and expansion.[29]

There are other models which encompass the therapeutic but have a wider frame of reference, and these may operate within church gatherings.

The Revd Tim Stead is an Anglican rector in Oxford. He tells us that he has been in ministry for twenty years and that he is an accredited teacher of Mindfulness Based Cognitive Therapy. For the past four years he has run a weekly drop-in session, courses for clergy, and retreats. He told us this about the weekly drop-in session, 'We have one guided mindfulness meditation for 30 minutes and one silent meditation for 30 minutes. Once a month I contribute some teaching input. This is turning into a small community in itself with many members not regular churchgoers but who are happy to join this event led by an Anglican vicar – interesting! We also have a meal together once a term.' The evening normally starts with a cup of tea and there is a community break between the guided and silent meditation sessions.

The essence of what he teaches is that 'you are learning a new skill which enables you to live every moment more fully, more joyfully and more compassionately in the present with full awareness and without crippling self-judgment. Simple eh?! Well, not so simple actually since our minds tend (some more than others) to spend so much of our time fretting over the past or worrying about the future – or even without the fretting or worrying, planning and scheming to manipulate the world around us better to fit what we would like it to be ... Mindfulness, then, has been shown not only to reduce stress which complicates so many personal and medical conditions but also to help us to open up more fully to the whole of life and all that is happening or being offered to us in it. Quite simply it is offering us a more awake and alive way to go about living.'

His new book *Mindfulness and Christian Spirituality* sets out his understanding.[30]

Shaun Lambert is Senior Minister at Stanmore Baptist

MEDITATION

Church, London, and is working on a doctoral thesis on Mindfulness. He has written *A Book of Sparks*, which is a study in a Christian understanding of Mindfulness.[31] He has developed a model that encompasses various ways of drawing Christians and non-churchgoers together. He also operates a cafe in the ministry:

'I run Mindful Church Café in a local coffee shop called Costa. Costa provides baristas and we run between 6.30 and 8.30 p.m. after hours. I cover topics like health, stress, parenting, relationships, wisdom, creativity drawing on the wisdom of psychology and theology, tapping into the burgeoning interest in natural spirituality and spiritual practices in our culture.

It is interactive and not passive in style. There is an opportunity to engage with mindful awareness practices, including mindful reading, mindful walking, compassion meditations, and chocolate meditations! Some of these come out of natural embodied mindfulness or awareness and some are from secular psychology or Christian contemplative practices.

I might offer a choice in mindful reading, offering a passage of scripture to read slowly or a poem, and give people the chance to choose which one to do, as we always have a mixed group of those with faith and those without. Out of passages like the Seed and the Sower in Mark 4 comes another practice which is mindful or attentive listening, whether to God or to others. Mindful listening is about being fully present as we listen, and sustaining that. If our mind wanders we learn to direct it back to the focus of our attention.

Mindfulness of God is a form of contemplative evangelism, and I believe there is a huge untapped potential in this area. People from outside the church from different faith and ethnic backgrounds have come to the evenings.'

Mindful exercises that are used, like eating and walking, are to ensure we are in the present and not distracted by intrusive thoughts about the past or future. A mindful walk, for example, involves attentiveness to posture and movement. One must be upright but not stiff. Begin a step with the left foot, and walk at a steady pace but going slowly. In all of this one may be mindful of God's creation rather than being distracted by life's worries.[32] Mindful eating involves both attention, where one notices and enjoys food, and intention, where one eats with care for self. It entails being in the present moment.[33]

Meditation practices like mindfulness are for many an important part of who they are, and are as common as yoga classes. Whatever our initial thoughts about them are, we do have to seriously consider our response as 'taboo or to do?'

THINGS TO DO

As Mindfulness is so widespread, look at Guy Yeomans' church website. Consider his overview of meditation and consider its possible value for your church life and ministry. Look at other church or Christian groups in your community that decline to sponsor meditation sessions and explore with them the reasons for their reluctance.

START THE CONVERSATION

1. Take time to share with others about cases where you may have been involved in Mindfulness programmes or eastern mediation. Share where you are aware of its presence.
2. Reflect in your group on Psalm 1 and in light of this chapter ask what it is to meditate.
3. Phil Rickman's novel, *Midwinter of the Spirit*, has been made into an ITV television series. It explores the relationship between new age/eastern spirituality and spiritual warfare and traditional church life. Watch a couple of episodes and reflect on to what extent this represents the contemporary interest and confusion in society over meditation and other forms of spirituality.[34]

6
TRANSFORMATION MIND SEMINARS –
Are they my way or the 'highway'?

Frank Sinatra's signature song 'I did it my way' still resonates with many people. Lifestyle coaching and personal empowerment seminars are very common as a resource for equipping people to improve their relationships and careers. There are many seminar hosts who insist that we may transform our lives by taking control of the 'script' that is controlling us. Such seminars are found in public and church-based schools, para-church training, the workplace and vocational training, sports clinics and personal well-being events.

'I am learning to alter my perceptions and therefore change my 'reality' ... This was not easy when a mugger lunged at me on First Avenue with the clear intention of doing whatever he deemed necessary to get my handbag. I remember my flash reaction that I, by God, did not like playing the part of a victim. Instinctively I changed my 'part' and lunged back at him, shrieking like the Wicked Witch of the West until the mugger thought my insanity was something he didn't want to tangle with. I changed the script.'
Shirley Maclaine, *Going Within*
(New York: Bantam, 1989, 46 & 47).

John Kehoe was one of the father-figures of this movement and this was his punch-line message:

> Your mind creates your reality. You can choose to accept this or not. You can be conscious of it, and get your mind working for you, or you can ignore it, and allow it to work in ways that will hinder and hold you back. But your mind will always, and forever, be creating your reality.[1]

'Nothing can come into your experience unless you summon it through persistent thoughts.'

'An unlimited supply of ideas is available to you. All knowledge, discoveries, and inventions are in the Universal Mind as possibilities, waiting for the human mind to draw them forth. You hold everything in your consciousness.'

Rhonda Byrne, *The Secret* (New York, London, Toronto, Sydney: Atria Books, 2006), 43 &175.

We may illustrate the impact of these transformation mind seminars on church life through what has happened to some of our friends.

One was failing miserably at university and had a distant relationship with family and discontented with life. He ended up attending a seminar known as The Forum. In an intensive weekend gathering he learned that life is shaped by our own thoughts or script. If we think negative thoughts so our lives will be negative: we play the part of a victim. He found that message was what he needed to hear at that point in his life. The positive end result of the seminar was that he took responsibility for his studies and his family relationships. His grades improved and he was much closer to his family than before. His parents were Christians and they cried: his transformation was a 'miracle'. However, they wanted to understand how and why their son had changed. We encouraged them to visit an information session to discover more about the seminar. They came away disturbed by what they heard.

Even though he experienced some real positive changes, he gradually felt some unease about where he was headed. There seemed to be a few holes in explaining every success and failure simply through the slogan 'change your script'. He met some Christians who challenged him to think about who he was really becoming. Over a period of time of reflection he realised that the message of The Forum was deficient. He entered into a faith commitment and his life was remarkably changed to the point that he became a minister and then worked in a para-church ministry. The Forum had been a stepping stone on the road to faith.

A different story concerns an active Christian who had left Europe and migrated to Australia. She met and married a mutual Christian friend of ours. Sadly, within a year of being married their relationship was fracturing and they separated. We were naturally concerned about them and they individually reached out to us as listening friends. We urged her to seek some professional counselling assistance. A few months later she rang us one Sunday afternoon. She was talking to us during an interval period in a weekend Forum gathering! She swiftly apologised to us for her past behaviour and indicated that she was changing her script. She was taking responsibility and reorienting her thinking. Unfortunately, the changing of the script did not lead to reconciliation in the marriage. Instead, her new script led her to drift away from her estranged husband and church affiliations.

In popular spirituality the idea of mind power transformation has been expressed by authors such as Rhonda Byrne in *The Secret*. This attractional concept has had a global impact in books and seminars. In the discernment section we will discuss how this relates to the Christian prosperity gospel. Some of the best-known groups and instructors include: John Kehoe, Wayne Dyer, The Forum, London Magnetic Mind Power Mastery Group, Harry Palmer's Avatar Course, Delfin, Insight, Silva Mind Control, Superteaching.

BACKGROUND

The rise of mind power transformation owes a debt to a group known as New Thought that emerged in the 1870s in the USA. New Thought was spearheaded by P. P. Quimby. This non-Christian metaphysical group taught visualising health, wealth and power. At that time a number of other teachers emerged who pioneered some new religious groups and propagated ideas about the relationship between your thoughts and reality. These include Warren Felt Evans, Charles Fillmore, Ernest Holmes and Mary Baker Eddy (founder of Christian Science).

If you concentrate on positive thoughts you will experience positive outcomes; if you dwell on negative thoughts you will have bad experiences. If you concentrate your thoughts on creating prosperity and optimum health then you will become wealthy and healthy. The idea is that whatever your mind can conceive is something that you can achieve is a root principle.

If you are wondering if there is a direct connection between Mind Powers/Visualisation and the 'Name it and Claim it' or 'Word-Faith' message of some telepreachers, the answer is 'yes'. Kenneth Copeland a prominent leader of the Word-Faith movement, studied under Kenneth Hagin. Hagin was indebted in many ways to the writings of E. W. Kenyon. Kenyon hovered on the fringes of the early Pentecostal churches and he was directly influenced by Quimby. The classic historical study on New Thought is Charles Braden's *Spirits in Rebellion*. Dan R. McConnell's *A Different Gospel* which is based on his thesis at Oral Roberts University documented the connections between the writings of Kenyon and Hagin. The concerns raised by McConnell take on added importance when we recall that Oral Roberts University was established as a Pentecostal institution.

CONTACT POINTS

One of our major newspapers ran a series of articles on its concerns about transformation mind powers programmes being used as compulsory training for pupils in public schools. Students were encouraged to adopt a worldview which involved retreating to a quiet place to listen voices that they hear. We were aware that the designer of the programme was a new age guide who taught astral travelling. The concern was that the programme was endorsed by a leading church school whose Principal was an evangelical Christian. He had not discerned that the programme had these strong spiritual and mind power elements in them. Global financial magazines draw attention to professional development seminars which are compulsory for corporation leadership that feature pop spirituality beliefs and mind power practices. We know of instances where some Christians have felt compelled to challenge their employers in work place tribunals over the question of religious liberty versus compulsory indoctrination.

We are sometimes asked about *A Course in Miracles* if it is a mind powers programme. It is found in informal study groups that have formed in both church settings and outside the church. It does have as a key element the need to re-engineer beliefs that bind us in fear and failure, which is a common thread across all mind powers programmes. The Course does teach that there is a Universal Mind that we must connect with to become whole and complete persons. However, *A Course in Miracles* is much broader in its scope. One may study the text either individually or in a group setting.

A Course in Miracles was published in the mid-1970s and is divided into three parts: text, workbook, teacher's manual. The book is designed with exercises that last a whole year. The Course is a text that Helen Schucman claims she 'channelled' from an external source. The implied source is Jesus. The message is that we mistake this material world for reality and our ego as if it is our true nature. Instead our true identity is found in God and we discover through the Course that we are one with God. God is actually an impersonal mind. The Course also deals with misconceptions about guilt. The punch-line is there are two choices: love and fear. This choice involves the power of the mind to select the right path. What the Course's exercises facilitate is choosing love and in that process finding transformation.

The Course has sold over a million copies and it has inspired others who have written books based around it. Some of the best-known books are: Gerald Jampolsky, *Love Is Letting Go of Fear*; Kenneth Wapnick, *The Meaning of Forgiveness*; Marianne Williamson, *A Return to Love*.

DISCERNMENT

In transformation mind power seminars one finds three important techniques: creative visualisation, centring and Neurolinguistic Programming (NLP). Creative visualisation involves harnessing the power of thought to materialise as a reality in the physical world. For example, a sports coach may use a mental exercise to guide athletes envisaging an Olympic Games gold medal. Most golfers will play a difficult shot through their mind first before actually hitting the ball. The problem is where the visualisation is taken to be reality: not every competitor will receive a gold medal. This visualisation technique may be augmented by using self-hypnosis, forms of meditation, or through a mentor-guided exercise.

Centring is a technique for harmonising the left brain (analytical) and the right brain (intuitive). The point is made that we will be lopsided if one hemisphere of the brain overrides the other. The recommendation is that one needs harmony between the two hemispheres.

NLP is a form of educational psychology that focuses on three forms of communication and learning styles: those who learn by listening (auditory), those who learn via demonstrations (visual), and those who learn by doing (kinaesthetic). NLP also places an emphasis on understanding how we communicate besides using words and one learns to observe bodily movements and non-verbal cues. The general aim of NLP is by discovering these different styles of learning one may improve communication. In NLP one is also taught how to control the brain with the techniques of visualisation and centring instead of one's thoughts controlling how one lives.

Some Markers

There are markers that may be identified with some (but not all) transformational seminars

- The promise of unlimited success
- Large fees for attendees
- Visualisation is the key to success
- Positive affirmations where participants engage in reciting self-congratulatory statements
- Using particular types of 'New Age' tools for transformation such as chanting mantras, undertaking out-of-body soul travel, rebirthing sessions.
- The use of strong emotional confrontation to shatter self-images or preconceived beliefs.
- A subtle promise may be expressed that one may attain 'enlightenment' in the same way as the instructor or creator of the seminar.
- A seminar or workshop is conducted as a long intensive experience held over a weekend. There may be a strong authoritarian undercurrent in the words and actions of an instructor. In those contexts the seminars tend to deprive participants of sleep and regular meals. The aim is to break down critical thinking in favour of 'getting it' in a heightened state of emotional euphoria or vulnerability. What participants must grasp is that their mind creates their reality. Psychologists such as Louise Samways have raised valid concerns that this sort of group behaviour in decision-making may involve very manipulative and cultic overtones.[2] This is a fair warning for church camps, retreats and weekend house-parties to heed

where even with the best spiritual intentions an intense and unbalanced atmosphere of excitement may be created. Unless people are given sufficient time and space to rest, reflect and debrief in a peaceful and non-manipulative way, it is possible for people to be manipulated in the decisions and lifestyle outcomes they choose.

John Drane suggests that in a corporate public setting there are four fundamental cords that are not dissimilar to the above:

- Tendency to self-indulgence.
- Bias against rationality.
- Lack of reality ... for even supposing that any of this works, by definition only a minority can make it to the top of the corporate ladder.
- The market-driven incentive to make money.

The above was apparent to him in much of the culture of Wall Street before the global credit crash.[3]

Biblical reflection

Over the years we have found three biblical principles to be helpful in considering whether a transformational mind seminar, be it 'Christian' or otherwise, is taboo or to do. There is a clear need to maintain some balance about fallen humanity when seeking to motivate people to have healthy self-esteem and to think and act positively and creatively.

First, we must remember that we do not control everything. We interact with forces, circumstances, and suffer due to the actions of other agents. The Bible is full of stories that illustrate this such as the Good Samaritan. We also know of people who have bounced back from horrible experiences that were entirely due to external forces. A passage that is often taken as supporting mind power is from Proverbs 23:7, 'as a person thinks, so they are'. In context the passage has nothing to do with your mind creating reality. It is about a stingy host who is more concerned with the price-tag of the dinner and is only offering scraps on a plate. The verse is a warning about Scrooge-like characters.

Second, God is ultimately in control. God does invite us into a relationship where we discover who we really are and who we might become if we turn away from self-centredness. The great 'risk' is surrendering our 'control' into the hands of the One who created us and who will guide us through life. One noticeable gap in most transformation seminars is the understanding that God knows us and has providential care: 'Before I formed you in the womb I knew you, and before you were born I consecrated you' (Jer. 1:5).

Third, Jesus modelled the challenging and costly path of servanthood as the way to empowerment and fulfilment. Jesus' way is not a self-focus approach. The story of the Good Samaritan illustrates that servanthood is the way and tragically the two religious characters of the story avoided the injured man.

A holistic understanding of the place of God's promises in scripture, such as all things working together for good (Rom. 8:28), need to be kept in view too. Many mainline churches have excelled in expositing passages without developing some clear practical advice on how to act on God's assurances in our personal development and spiritual journey. In this respect the Word-Faith movement has entered that gap with an uncluttered emphasis of living by God's promises. This has encouraged many to see God involved in their ordinary daily life. People have sought a better sense of self-worth, improving personal relationships, healing and trusting God for what we need.

People today are asking two things about a worldview: is it true? and does it work? The Word-Faith incentives to trust God's assurances has not been kept under the canopy of the above three principles. Perhaps the lesson about a balanced way is (a) for mainline churches is to rediscover balance and empowered living while (b) for the Word-Faith churches it is the need to rediscover the three main biblical principles as a grid for Christian discipleship.

TABOO OR TO DO?

Vocation

Transformation mind power seminars have spawned a movement that mentors and life-coaches have been using to reorient the way we think, compete and work. It has consequently found itself in the world of vocation and is having a profound influence. Mentors and life-coaches may be great motivators who urge us to succeed. They play a positive role in the workplace and in other settings. This is a field where Christian mentors play a good role in discerning a proper understanding of vocation.

The excesses and extremes of the Mind Powers movement may be countered by thinking more carefully about a Christian approach to vocation. It is essential that we reframe the current movements that are shaping the dialogue on vocation. We suggest below a few points about recovering a biblical understanding of vocation that is illustrated by a case that transformed one particular workplace and has had a global impact.

Some Christians have assumed that the only authentic godly vocation is to be ordained to the ministry, or to be a missionary living overseas, or to join a monastic order. This view tends to regard any other kind of work as merely a means to an end: earn wages for work in order to purchase the necessary goods for daily survival. A hard-nosed attitude about making money seems to dominate the public and corporate sector and squashes any idea that work should be enjoyable and that workers may feel they are making a meaningful contribution to the lives of others.

A biblical understanding of work is that God ordained it in Eden as something that was positive and meaningful. Humans were invited to become co-workers so that the whole creation should flourish to God's glory and praise. God blessed the task of working in the creation (Gen. 1:26-28; 2:15). Vocation was not meant to be drudgery or just a means to an end in daily survival. Unfortunately human sinfulness has thrown a proverbial 'spanner in the works'. Work is burdened by the consequences of sin (Gen. 3:19). The things that God made were designed to function well but are now frustrated by our sinfulness and everything waits for the resurrected Christ to liberate the entire creation (Rom. 8:19-22).

In our technologically-driven age employees may feel at times that they are stifled in their creativity by work-processes that seem dehumanising. We may feel metaphorically cramped by working inside what seems like the equivalent of an iron cage.

The Christian understanding of vocation builds on the original blessing of work in Eden through the doctrine that all believers are servants and priests of the risen Christ. Vocation then involves turning aside from being me-centred, which is rife today, over to a concern for one's neighbour (fellow workers and the community at large) and even for God's creation. Our everyday work activities present us with the opportunity to be of service to others. If we are assured of God's grace abounding in our lives and in the creation then we may enter into the workplace as servants.

We will daily face the push-pull effects of secular values that would call us to compromise our calling before God. We must be discerning that we do not succumb to what is unethical and soul-destroying. Instead, we must become God's salt that flavours and seasons the workplace for the glory of Christ Jesus (Col. 3:17): caring for our neighbours, seeking to be peace-makers, pursuing justice where necessary, blessing others and the creation by our deeds.

One striking story that illustrates this is Wayne Alderson's impact on changing relationships between management and labour in the USA. Alderson (1926-2013) was the son of a coalminer and at age eighteen enlisted for service during the Second World War. In the battles against German troops, Alderson won a Purple Heart medal.[4]

After the war he studied for a business degree and by the late 1960s he had moved up through the ranks at Pittron a steel foundry. Sadly the relations between labour and management were threadbare and in a chain of turbulent events the workers went on strike. Alderson met a delegation of a half-a-dozen workers at a Holiday Inn where there were harsh words and threats exchanged.

The tension broke as Alderson stood his ground and after a moment he had won their trust.

Back at the steel mill Alderson decided to breach the gulf between labour and management. He started a voluntary Bible study with some of the workers and it didn't take long before individual relationships improved. He also made the effort to become genuinely acquainted with the foundry workers and to understand the difficult conditions under which they worked. The problems at the foundry were dramatically turned around as Alderson began applying principles that cultivate human dignity: giving love, dignity and respect to the workers. The mill went from the brink of bankruptcy and total worker revolt and within a few short years was operating at a profit.

What happened at the mill inspired Alderson, along with his daughter Nancy, to widen the horizons for the rest of corporate America. The Value of the Person movement was born and Alderson's story inspired the book *Stronger Than Steel*.[5] As a small ripple began spreading through different business sectors, the story reached across to Marxist Poland to inspire Lech Walesa who was the leader of the Solidarity movement.[6] It has reached into the strife-torn area of northern Uganda.[7]

Alderson's story presents four coaching goals for managers to act on:

- Know the faces and names of employees.
- Communicate positive attitudes with words and actions.
- Understand non-verbal communication (body language).
- Create a good mood that motivates employees.

CASE STUDIES

We have been consulted by employees in private and public sector, as well as teachers and students in schools, over whether the transformation seminars are taboo or to do, especially when attendance is compulsory. In fact in some cases this has resulted in employees seeking formal advice from lawyers who specialise in work-place law on how to protect their employment and status.

We have pointed out that some seminars are at best ideologically-based and some have a religious ethos. We are aware that legislators in a number of jurisdictions are grappling with work-place laws in light of these seminars. It has been noted that one should not be 'forced' to attend. It is important for churches to work constructively through these issues. We have found by discussing these matters in church forums that people are able to work out the critical issues as they apply to employment, education, and mentoring others.

In new spirituality festivals one finds various exhibitors who offer transformational seminars for work and lifestyle matters. Exhibitors have finely-honed sales-skills and endeavour to persuade visitors to sign up for an information session. Their 'sales pitch' is unmistakeable with slogans used that emphasise empowerment and success. This is a constructive place for the church to be engaged in mission. We and others have created banners or leaflets with helpful affirmations that reflect a biblical outlook that is positive but different from other festival offerings. Mentors and life-coaches have found these affirmations as transferable concepts:

I affirm that transforming/refocusing my goals begins with the renewing of the mind.

I affirm that I am special, created in God's image, and have been given tremendous capabilities. I will positively use my gifts, intuition, and creativity.

I affirm that I am dependent on circumstances, others, and God for life's fulfilment. This is a beautiful concept and is in touch with reality.

I affirm that I am a shamrock of body, mind, and spirit. I only operate as a wholly integrated person when energized by the one who is beyond us, yet near enough to personally comfort, guide, and strengthen us.

I affirm that love is more powerful than dreams.

I affirm that servanthood and dying for others is the authentic path. I conceive people, families, and nations growing together in mutual service.

In conversations that often follow there is opportunity for prayer and general discussions about how one handles the rollercoaster of life. These points and the accompanying biblical passages do connect with the spiritual seeker, especially those who are exploring stages of life changes:

- Have balanced goals (Mat. 6:25)
- Don't keep anxieties to yourself (Gal. 6:2)
- Be aware that God cares (Matt. 6:26)
- Trust the power of prayer (Phil. 4:6-7)

There are also the old homespun remedies such as 'pat your dog' and 'dig in the garden!'

Sports, military and corporate chaplains often lead the way in missional ministry. They are aware of the influence of transformation mind powers and the need to creatively interact with the Christian worldview as they minister on the coal-face. A classic illustration comes from some years ago from our colleague Father John Woods. He handed a personal note to the captain of a football team that he was engaged with. John does not believe that prayer wins football matches but had a sense that his letter had a life of its own. The press would later report that the players said that the chaplain's letter had been a motivating force for them. As a goal was kicked that tied the game and a victory try was scored in extra time the key players involved indicated that the chaplain's letter was in their thoughts. This was the team's first grand final win and the letter was read out by the captain before they ran on-field. John wrote:

Just a note to wish you and the other guys all the very best for Sunday. I consider it a privilege to have been associated with you as Chaplain over the years. These sentiments would be echoed by your families, friends and many thousands of fans. Simply stated, the Grand Final is a challenge for you to realise your God-given potential as footballers. Inside each of you is a dream. Dreams do come true if you are willing to sacrifice what you are to become what your dream calls you to be. My prayer for you is that of St Paul: 'May your hidden self grow strong.' May it be a great game played in the true spirit of the occasion. Good luck. God bless and see you Sunday.

Michael Graham's life-story is truly fascinating. He was once part of the mind powers world and the world of Indian spiritual leaders. Today he operates in India and models a missional approach there which involves living and ministering among followers of gurus such as Bhagwan Shree Rajneesh, Sai Baba and Swami Muktananda. He mentors a new generation of followers of Jesus whose spiritual journey began with such movements. His model is a challenge for us to incarnate into this world at home or overseas.

Michael grew up in Australia and very early on was fascinated with yoga and meditation. This interest led him on a journey of self-discovery and truth-quest spanning twenty-eight years that took him to India. It also drew him into the high levels of corporate re-engineering as he was trained by several mind power and personal transformation groups: Silva Mind Control, the Forum, Avatar, and the Hoffman Quadrinity Process.

Michael noted that while there were many creative effects generated in human potential seminars and workshops, he still did not experience any profound personal renewal or transformation. He reached a desolate point in life and decided he would try and crack the spiritual-transformational barrier in an intensive isolated meditative retreat. During that time he had an unexpected mystical encounter with the resurrected Christ. He discovered the transforming power of God's forgiveness and grace.[8] He finds the uniqueness that resonates and attracts is the release from striving through reliance on God's grace.

People today are seeking to be the best person they can possibly be. That hunger may very well lead them to transformational mind powers. Discernment is needed by the church. There is clearly an opportunity for a bridge to be built. There will be instances of things that are taboo but also positive things to do.

THINGS TO DO

Look at the seminars you are invited to in your work-place and ascertain to what extent transformational mind powers sessions are being offered. Peruse the trade and professional magazines your office subscribes to and spot the articles and advertisements for transformational seminars. Those who are involved in education could look at the self-improvement courses that are on offer for schools, teachers, high-school students and parents. Review the books and magazines you read regularly about lifestyle and leisure to discern the influence of transformational mind powers.
If you are an entrepreneur, life-coach or business leader consider ways in which you may develop seminars or workshops that respects the human dignity and potential of all people but without the pitfalls of mind powers.

START THE CONVERSATION

1. In your group talk about any experiences that you have had with transformational mind powers seminars.
2. What are the ways in which your church could reach out to people who are seeking to be the best possible person they can be in their work, recreation and relationships?
3. Find a book about vocation and success that will be a good 'book-club' conversation starter.
4. If you are a pastor or bible study group leader encourage a group forum to explore the Word-Faith and transformational mind powers worldviews.
5. Consider handing the prayer of Father John Woods to your local coach or sports co-ordinator.

7
ANGELS AND SPIRIT GUIDES –
Connect or disconnect?

Today people are very open to having encounters with angels in their spiritual search. The evidence for this is abundant with angel calendars, figurines, books recounting stories of angel encounters, and angels in television shows. A deeper concern for angels is seen in cases where healing practitioners consult angelic guides. The practitioner emphasises that the process involves meeting an angel or spirit guide who talks to you, and assists you in healing and empowerment. A classic case is with the alternate spiritual community of Findhorn, Scotland, where there is collaboration with agricultural angels in developing the crops and garden.

We have found that, even though our Christian art, church stained glass windows and literature dramatically display angels, there seems to be at times greater appreciation of the reality of angels outside the church than within. In this book we have highlighted that those who are 'spiritual but not religious' are quite open to exploring things that are not easily explained through science. The failure of materialism and technology to make us feel complete has meant that the supernatural is back on the agenda. As in ages past when life's circumstances were harsh and we could feel vulnerable on our own without heavenly witnesses, we are looking for hope in all areas of life. New

Spirituality writer Sophy Burnham affirms, 'No one who has seen an angel ever mistakes it for a ghost. Angels are remarkable for their warmth and light, and all who see them speak in awe of their iridescent and refulgent light, of brilliant colours, or else of the unbearable whiteness of their being. You are flooded with laughter, happiness.'[1]

We were watching a documentary on experimenting with spiritual disciplines for healing. The documentary featured an indigenous woman who had had a background in a Pentecostal church but was no longer part of it. The woman was seeking release from her childhood experience of sexual abuse. A spiritual theatre workshop offered a way of acting out her need for release from the bondage of the past. She lay on the floor cowering under some chairs to illustrate her fear of being assaulted. To one side of the theatre were two people playing the role of angels. The indigenous lady called out for the angels to come and rescue her. As they stepped forward and reached out to lift her up from under the chairs she said, 'I need the angels to help me because they have nothing to do with God.' Her startling words struck us as being a comment about her belief that angels are religiously neutral and friendly beings. She said that her church experiences had left her with negative impressions from people who had held to a very harsh understanding of who God is.

At Christmas time there is much emphasis in churches on angels involved in the birth of Jesus. What seems odd is that, apart from Christmas, we tend to suffer from amnesia about angels in the rest of Jesus' life and throughout the Bible. In light of the renewed interest in angels is it time for churches to reconnect with narratives about angels in our lives? We may need to speak about their presence and participation in our story. As we will see from the case studies, there are those who want to keep angels in the background for fear that too much interest may take us away from being centred on Jesus Christ. This reaction is almost like the early Puritan settlers in America who downplayed all feast days except for the Sabbath.[2] Again, the question is 'taboo or to do?'

BACKGROUND

Angels are present in many religious traditions such as Zoroastrianism, Hinduism, Judaism, Christianity, and Islam. In the Hindu tradition such beings are known as devas. Devas were deities in earliest Hindu Vedic belief but, as the religion developed, they were replaced in importance by other gods. Devas are regarded as demi-god figures whose functions are similar to those of angelic messengers.

The three faiths that give angels the most attention are Judaism, Christianity, and Islam. We will briefly explore these three, and then consider how the fascination with angels has moved from these traditions and surfaced in contemporary 'spiritual but not religious' beliefs.

> 'Zoroastrianism, Judaism, Christianity, Islam…have not known how to tell the story of their truths without angelic intercessions, nor is there any major religious tradition, Eastern or Western, that does not rely upon angels. The spiritual life, whether expressed in worship and prayer, in private contemplation, or in the arts, needs some kind of vision of the angels. That vision burgeons in some eras and falls away in others, yet on some level it generally abides.'
>
> Harold Bloom, *Omens of Millennium: The Gnosis of Angels, Dreams and Resurrection* (London: Fourth Estate, 1997), 167.

Islam
In Islam angels are integral to faith, and are second only in belief to Allah (God). It is stated angels are chiefly engaged in the worship and service of God and act as messengers between Allah and humans. They are created from light or fire. They neither eat nor sleep, and exist to praise Allah. They appear in human form on earth but have an unseen form in heaven. The prophet Muhammad had angelic

encounters as Gabriel (Djibril) spoke the words of Allah that are recorded in the Qur'an as divine revelation. Gabriel accompanied Muhammad on his mystical night journey to heaven.

The Qur'an mentions other angels such as Michael (Mikhail) the angel of providence, Israfil, the angel who summons us to the resurrection, and Izra'il the angel of death. Other angels act as protectors, particularly to guard humans from the deceptive spirits or demons known as the jinn. Angels also guard holy sites such as the Ka'aba in Mecca which is a focal point for the annual pilgrimage to Mecca. The angels Munkir and Nakir come to the graves and pose questions of faith. The true believers are given glimpses of Paradise, while evil-doers are shown hell. Angels also bear witness to the faithful in prayer times, when sermons are preached and when the Qur'an is read aloud.

Another important angelic figure is Iblis or Shaitaan who is the Islamic equivalent of the Devil. Iblis directly disobeyed Allah and was banished from heaven. He is permitted to exist and, along with his earthly followers, will face punishment on the Day of Judgment.

Judaism

Judaism gives prominence to angels partly because of their place in the Bible, which we will explore in our section on Christianity. Angels have also featured in synagogue art in history, and are mentioned at length in different parts of the Talmud. The Talmud is a body of writings that contains the teachings and commentaries of rabbis. In the Talmud the rabbis refer to a division between peaceful and evil angels. The best known include the four archangels: Gabriel, Michael, Uriel, Raphael. Another important angel is Metatron.

According to the Talmud the angels are numberless and some rabbis speculated that God made new batches of angels every day. Some rabbis taught that there are both eternal angels and others that are temporal or mortal. There is also an understanding that there are ranks or classes of angels. Today the Hasidic Jews hold to a literal belief in angels while among those who belong to the Orthodox and Reform schools of Judaism they tend to be regardedas symbolic.

ANGELS AND SPIRIT GUIDES

Christianity

A noticeable feature about the Bible is that angels are involved from the beginning (Gen. 3:24), to the end, appearing throughout the Book of Revelation where, in the last chapter, an angel discusses truth with the apostle John (22: 7). Angels appear throughout Jesus' life. Luke records them being present to announce his conception and birth (Luke 1-2), at his temptation (Luke 4), during his agonising last prayer before death (Luke 22:43), announcing his resurrection (Mark 16:4-7), on his return to heaven (Acts 1:10-11) and being the army of his second coming (Rev 19:11-18).

There are three hundred biblical references to angels, and a helpful way of exploring the topic is to sort the biblical passages into three categories: *nature, organisation*, and *tasks*. As to their *nature*, angels are created beings (Psalm 148:1-5), and ministering spirits (Heb. 1:14). Though they are spirits they may appear in human form (Luke 1-2). They are intelligent (2 Sam. 14:20), have free will (Jude 6) and neither marry nor die (Luke 20:34-36).

As to their *organisation*, God is their head (Psalm 148:1-5) and they make up a heavenly court comprising the Archangel Michael (Jude 6); the 'Ambassador', Gabriel (Luke 1:26). There are guards called the Cherubim (Ezek. 10); servants of God, the Seraphs (Isaiah 6); and the heavenly hosts (Luke 2:13).

As to their *tasks* they praise God (Rev. 5:1-11), are God's messengers (Numbers 22:21-35; Matt. 1:20-21) and rejoice over our salvation (Luke 15:10). They serve us (Heb. 1:14), can bring strength to us (Luke 22:43) and protect us (Gen. 19:1-22; Ps. 34:7; 2 Kings 6:8-17). They are seen as advocates for children. The belief in guardian angels has a strong history in certain sections of the church, such as the Catholic tradition. Apart from a text in Matthew (18:10), there is some biblical evidence that supports this hope:

> For he will command his angels concerning you, to guard you in all your ways. On their hands they will bear you up, lest you strike your foot against a stone. (Psalm 91:11-12).

They are involved with the nations (Daniel 6), and sometimes bring answers to prayer (Daniel 10). Some Christians have inferred from Daniel 6 and Mark 5:10 that angels, particularly dark angels, are linked with geographical territories. Apart from these passages on biblical spiritual conflict, there is little biblical evidence to support claims about territorial spirits. The topic requires discernment, particularly to ensure that we do not concentrate more on demons than on the victory of the Risen Christ over all powers.

They also convey us to the other side (Luke 16:22). We are not alone in having family members who as they passed away said, 'The angels have come to take me to Jesus.' A dramatic story that has come to light in recent years concerns the fate of five missionaries in Ecuador. The missionaries made contact with the Huaorani people in the Auca territory. Unfortunately, the missionaries were speared to death due to a misunderstanding that arose between the tribe and the missionaries. Later, some female relatives of the dead missionaries went to live with the Huaorani people, and many came to faith in God. Steve Saint, a son of one of the deceased missionaries, had conversations with some of the tribesmen who had witnessed their slaying. They related that as the men died, they heard music and the sound of a choir. There were strange figures seen above the trees and along the ridge, and there was talk of moving lights and the sky full of 'fire flies'. The tribesmen were scared because it felt supernatural. Steve Saint has pondered about his father dying in the company of angels.[3]

Angels have featured in Christian art. For example, one famous biblical episode is in Numbers 22:22-27 where an angry Balaam beats his donkey and an angel intervenes. A fourth-century fresco found in the Catacomb of the Via Dino Compagni shows this incident. The story of Balaam returned to prominence in Christian art in the seventeenth century. The Dutch artist, Pieter Pieterszoon Lastman (1583-1633), painted this scene in 1622 and it now hangs in the Israel Museum in Jerusalem. Rembrandt Harmenszoon van Rijn (1606-1669) ranks as one of the world's greatest artists and one of his earliest paintings is *The*

Ass of Balaam balking before the Angel (1626) which belongs to the Musée Cognacq-Jay in Paris.

Spiritual but Not Religious

Philip has an interesting life-story encounter. When he and his wife Ruth were house-hunting they spotted a 'for sale' sign. The owner, Gina, was selling her home without using an agent. When they knocked on the door her first words were, 'I don't know about you but for me this is a very spiritual experience.' She invited them in and she said, 'It's so exciting for me to wake up every morning and to see angels on the ceiling.' They followed her to her bedroom and the plaster ceiling had cherubs. Philip noticed that there was a pile of books next to her bed by alternate spirituality writers such as Deepak Chopra, Shirley MacLaine, and Louise Hay.

Gina was of Greek ethnicity but she had been born in London's East End and spoke like a Cockney! Her interest in angels reflected quite a mix of sources: Greek Orthodox background; books about angels; other writings in alternate spirituality. Philip has had angel encounters, and so this was a natural point of contact for a fascinating conversation. Gina was excited by a common interest in spiritual things. She had had better offers for the house but decided to sell it to them because, in her words, they were 'spiritual people'!

Gina's interest in a smorgasbord approach to spiritual matters is similar to the experiences of many people today. They partake of things that have their roots in Judeo-Christian belief and in other sources. The alternate spiritual stream has been influenced by Emanuel Swedenborg's (1688-1772) mystical visions of heaven and angels. This led to the emergence of the Spiritualist churches in the nineteenth century that paid attention to angels and spirit guides. Also Madame Blavatsky (1831-1891) of the Theosophical Society borrowed the Hindu understanding of the devas and combined it with Christian ideas of angels. The views of Swedenborg and Blavatsky were rediscovered and popularised in the late twentieth century. In this regard they helped shape New Age thinking.

CONTACT POINTS

The contact points about angels will emerge in conversations, counselling services, festivals, school and community Christmas pageants. They come in unexpected ways. Alternate spirituality seekers and authors are happy to refer to the Bible on the topic of angels, more so than any other use of the Bible.

Consider the story of Gerry. He attended a lunchtime meeting that his older brother had organised as a Christian outreach on alternate spirituality. The topic of angels surfaced in the presentation. Philip was the speaker. Afterwards Gerry wanted a second opinion from Philip of an experience he had had. Before he became a follower of Jesus, Gerry had been experimenting with vision quests under the guidance of a mentor. Gerry's mentor gave him a task: he was to spend time over a forty-day period taking an astral travel with the goal of meeting an angel. Astral travel involves leaving one's body in a trance or dream and journeying in spiritual realms.

During the course of his vision quest Gerry encountered a being who called himself Michael. Michael said he was an angel and he had urgent advice for Gerry. Michael said, 'Stop all astral travelling. Follow Jesus.' After returning to his body Gerry read the gospels. What he had been seeking in astral travels was fulfilled by following Jesus. He asked, 'Was this a true angel sent by God?' The surprising thing is that Gerry's older brother was standing beside him as he told his story. His brother could not accept that God would send an angel to somebody doing astral travel: This had to be evil or a delusion. Gerry's brother was a victim of embracing the flaw of the excluded middle, which is a concept we discuss below.

DISCERNMENT

In this book we are not just inviting discernment with respect to other religious practices and belief. This is also a time when followers of Jesus need to reflect on where we may have missed things or forgotten truths on the spiritual realm. It's time to reframe our worldview.

Paul Hiebert has urged us to be discerning and to open our eyes in a missional sense to the topic of angels. He said that in the West we have tended to operate with a two-tiered model involving just God and us. The influence of the Enlightenment, with its emphasis on scepticism, reason and scientific knowledge, on the Western church has led many of us to stop talking about the supernatural. We have 'apologised' for such quaint beliefs like angels. The 'God and us' outlook has diminished our worship as we tend to sing songs with lyrics that only refer to our praise and relationship with God. The Bible is adamant that we are members of a greater choir that encompasses angels and all of creation in praise (Psalm 19:1-4; 65:12-13; 69:34; 96:11-12; 98:7-8; 103:22; 145:10; 148; 1 Chron.16:31-32; Isa. 43:20; 44:23; 55:12; Rev. 5:13).

The idea that all creation may in its own way pray and praise its Creator has been practically inconceivable to many Christians throughout the centuries ... Prayer and praise are regularly defined as solely human activities abstracted from the world of fellow creatures. These omissions are testimony to a lack of imagination.

Andrew Linzey and Cohn-Sherbok, *After Noah: Animals and the Liberation of Theology* (London: Mowbray, 1997), 108.

Early church liturgies included angels and the rest of creation in its declarations of praise and worship. Understandably the Protestant Reformation placed great emphasis on our personal relationship with God. However, the early Protestant hymns did not overlook angels and creation. As we write this chapter, Christmas carols fill the air. We have forgotten that the beloved lyrics of Charles Wesley's 'Hark the Herald Angel Sings' originally contained this stanza about all of creation:

TABOO OR TO DO?

> Joyful, all ye nations, rise,
> Join the triumph of the skies;
> Universal nature say,
> 'Christ the Lord is born to-day!'

Another favourite is Isaac Watt's 'Joy to the World,' which is based on Psalm 98: 'heaven [angels] and nature sing' and the 'fields and floods, rocks, hills and plains repeat the sounding joy.'[4]

The two-tier view is in contrast with the biblical understanding of a middle-layer or level that involves the angelic and demonic. Hiebert calls the elimination of the middle layer the 'flaw of the excluded middle.'[4] A litmus test for this is to pick up handbooks on theology or doctrine and see if much is said about angels. He says that we Christians in the West need to open our eyes to the reality of angels. This is particularly so if we want to share our faith with people who are attracted to the 'spiritual but not religious.'

Edmund Spenser's *The Faerie Queen*

How oft do they their silver bowers leave, To come to succor us, that succor want?

How oft do they with golden pinions, cleave the fitting skies, like flying pursuivant,

Against foul fiends to aid us militant?

They for us fight, they watch and duly ward,

And their bright, squadrons round about us plant,

And all for love, and nothing for reward – O why should heavenly God to men have such regard?

(II.viii.2)

One way of applying this is to read 2 Kings 6, and ask 'Am I like Elisha or Elisha's servant?'. The story involves the prophet Elisha. The king of Aram (modern Syria), who believed Elisha was giving prophetic battle insights to Israel's king, was hunting him down. He needed to eliminate Elisha and win the war against Israel. His scouts located Elisha at Dothan and the king of Aram surrounded his camp with a multitude of soldiers. Elisha's servant rose early in the morning, went out and saw the troops. He panicked and badgered the prophet, 'What shall we do?' Elisha answered, 'Do not be afraid, for those who are with us are more than those who are with them.' Elisha then prayed, 'O Lord, please open his eyes that he may see.' The servant's eyes were opened and he saw 'the mountain was full of horses and chariots of fire all around Elisha'. He saw the heavenly host of angels sent to protect them.

When conducting a seminar on spirituality at a music festival a woman spoke to us about her struggles with astral travel. She became so absorbed with astral travelling that after a time it made her feel very uneasy. She was distressed because the experiences became involuntary. The crunch-time for her came when a spirit guide woke her up. While she hovered above her body, a dark entity assaulted her body. She found release from astral travels when several Christians prayed for her. Sometime later Ross recounted this story on a secular radio station on a special segment on spiritual encounters today. There was a positive response from the listening audience. However a number suggested that she should have prayed before her astral travels that only good angels would accompany her. There was a general consensus that there are both friendly and hostile spirits. Conversations like these should prompt us to stop demythologising our faith of supernatural elements including angels. If we don't we should not be surprised that alternatives appear in a spiritually searching age. By myth we are not saying that events in the Bible are fictitious or non-historical.

This story is also a helpful reminder that when we meet people who are open to angels and spirit guides, we need to exercise discernment about the reality of malevolent beings (Rev. 12:1-13; Eph. 6:12). We have discussed this problem in our chapter on Hallowe'en. The key to angelic blessing is to focus on Jesus who is superior to, and worshipped by the angels. With Jesus at the centre the possibility of angelic blessings then makes sense (Eph. 1:3).

We are often asked should we make contact with angels or

heavenly beings as part of our journey. There is an angelic guide movement that centres attention on the role of angels speaking to us, bringing guidance and healing. This movement has influenced both alternate spirituality groups, with the message shared in festivals and exhibitions, and also parts of the Church. They often connect angels to Reiki healing or other energy healing.

The Bible does tell stories where angels spoke directly to guide central characters such as Abraham, Jacob, Moses, Daniel, Joseph, Mary, and John. Philip has had at least three angel encounters that brought him healing, and on one occasion was desperately lost and an angel 'rescued' him with specific directions that took him out of harm's way. The figure vanished after the assistance.[5] As we have indicated in the story of Gerry, these special encounters continue today in pointing people to Jesus. It is not uncommon to hear stories of angelic guidance in Muslim and New Spirituality conversions. In our experience God can move in mysterious ways.

While Christian living should open our eyes to the possibility of 'entertaining angels unaware' (Heb. 13:2), we should be discerning. Our discipleship focus is on growth and equipping through the Word of God, as together we follow the guidance of the Holy Spirit. It's the voice of Jesus that we depend on, and do not harden our hearts against (Heb. 13:7). He is our life and message. This same principle applies to following 'gurus' such as Jonathan Edwards who insist that we listen to voices from the other side.

CASE STUDIES

In our experience interactive sermons and bible studies that feature angels are informative and enriching for our life. People like to talk about angels. It is often the case that people open up about their angel stories. A conversational, community preaching approach invites people in advance of the event, from the church and broader community, to pose their questions, and to share their angel experiences. Sermon titles that 'work' include 'All You Want to Know About Angels,' 'Friends in High Places', to the more provocative title 'How to have angels empower your life'. The latter title suits missional contexts. The aim is to ensure that with eyes wide open to the spiritual realm that the focus is on the person of Jesus.

A talk that we have found helpful in a number of environments has the following structure. The introduction sets out our common interest in angels today with possibly some local testimonies about angels. After the introduction the talk covers remembering the Bible, where passages about angels are explored.

The next section is why is it that many of us are uneasy talking about angels. The final section examines how to live a life with eyes wide open, where angels are part of God's provision. We have relied on the material above about angels in preparing talks.[6]

Another approach is in the church pageant. In this age of dress-up as seen in fans of *Star Wars* and *Frozen*, the opportunity for playing out the biblical story is golden. It is like returning to the villages of the medieval ages where biblical pageants were a regular part of life, and the villagers were actively involved in the spectacle.

Ross was invited to speak at a church outreach Christmas pageant. The service was focused on the children and parents that had links to the church via its child day-care centre, play groups, Sunday School, and youth groups. However, angels were taboo. A month beforehand the minister asked Ross what was his chosen topic. Ross said it would be angels because this is a great connection point for the general community. He was bluntly told that topic would be unacceptable because he had banned angels from the pageant. We must, he said, get away from all the commercial trappings and centre on Jesus. Ross explained that angels were in the Christmas story, and gave the direction of the message. The minister relented. Before the service started he issued an apology to everyone for having banned the angels from the pageant, and acknowledged he had over-reacted. The apology created a positive effect among those present. Angels in church dramas, plays and pageants throughout the calendar have a significant part to play, particularly in connecting with the 'Spiritual but not religious'. It also reminds us of God's spiritual protection and provision.

In its glory days the Crystal Cathedral did this so well in its Easter and Christmas services, and followed the biblical text. The role of angels was dramatically played by actors who were hooked to wires and moved through the air above the congregation. These services were brilliantly done and faithful to the biblical text, and they appealed to thousands of people who attended.

In our chapter on Hallowe'en we mentioned that halos and angels may be featured in alternative events.

The theme of angels as messengers, who can play a unique role in our life, is a connecting point in spiritual festivals and exhibitions. The festivals have a strong appeal for women. We have decorated a booth with angel posters with the caption 'Friends in High Places'. We distributed a pamphlet 'The Rustle of Wings' which was very popular. It began with 'Angels and Us' which briefly recounted some angel stories. The next part outlined the heavenly origins of angels, and was followed by 'Angels and our spiritual quest'. Conversations in the exhibitor's booth allowed people to share their stories, as well as using a 'prayer-chair' for healing and guidance.

We found it was good to consolidate on the visitors' interest by inviting them to a post-festival seminar on angels. It created the space where relationships deepened. The interactive seminar expanded on the topics from the leaflet, including positive testimonies, discussion of stories, and concluded by pointing to Jesus as the one who is superior and in command of angels.

Angels may also be explored by letter-box drops inviting the local community to write in with their stories and questions. The same approach can be adapted to social media sites. We have found that this works well on local or mainstream radio programmes where the listening audience is invited to call-in and share their stories. People, who might not normally make contact with a church, and followers of Jesus, take the opportunity to open up. We vividly remember one caller telling us that he was a semi-trailer driver. He sounded like the salt-of-the-earth type of guy. He was travelling too quickly down a suburban street with a sharp incline and he saw a child walk out into the road. To his amazement a figure flashed in front of his truck and removed the child from the threat of his vehicle. When he pulled the vehicle to a halt he was trembling and in awe. This non-churchgoer kept on saying, 'it was an angel!' We continue to receive letters from people months after we have raised the topic in a public forum. People want to tell their stories and have conversations.

The topic of angels is not about 'Christianising' a matter that has intruded on the church. Instead it is more about rediscovering the place of angels in our lives, and reimagining how angels may play a part in our spiritual discipline and missional efforts to reach into the lives of others.

THINGS TO DO

Read 2 Kings 6:8-23. Take time to settle into the scene, to involve your senses and identify with the characters and events. Which characters do you relate to? What in your life makes you feel 'surrounded' by trouble? Are your eyes open to God's provision of protection and deliverance?

START THE CONVERSATION

1. Have you ever had an angel encounter? Share a story you know about where angels helped people. Take time to reflect on how the story's details make a difference to your understanding of life's journey.
2. In your group discuss why you think there is widespread interest in angels today? Take time to visit your local bookstores and malls and see what materials you find about angels.

3. Does your group or local church regularly include angels in the prayers and praise times? If your group does not, explore the reasons why this is so. Consider practical ways in which your group could include references to angels.

4. Mention was made in the chapter of Wesley's 'Hark the Herald Angels Sing' and Watts' 'Joy to the World'. Take time to examine your group or church's song-books and see how many songs/hymns include angels and the rest of creation in the praise of God. Discuss with the worship team about how frequent or infrequent songs about angels and creation's praise are used in your services.

8
ASTROLOGY, TAROT AND NUMEROLOGY –
Forbidden paths or helpful bridges?

One of the privileges we have is delivering seminars on spirituality and the search for meaning today. Ross was teaching a course on the post-Christendom search at Carson-Newman, a Christian University in Tennessee. He organised, as part of the programme, a group visit to Ashville in North Carolina. Ashville is perched in the mountains and is well known for its openness to Eastern religions and new spirituality practices. Before the field trip Ross reconnoitred the local 'new age' stores and the public square where spiritual seekers gather with their drums for the weekly gathering known as 'beating of the drums'. He popped into an organic cafe and found himself sitting next to two women, mother and daughter. When his eggs arrived the mother asked, 'how did you get yours so quickly, we were here before you and they haven't arrived?' The mother asked where Ross came from and what he was doing in America. She said she was a Baptist, and knew of Carson-Newman. She was puzzled as to why Ross was visiting a 'Pagan' town. He explained he was checking it out because he planned to bring students to Ashville and to explore connection points. She said, 'You're not a Christian!' Ross indicated that yes he is, and was looking at connecting people with God's love. She insisted, 'You're not a

Christian.' Ross tried to explain how the tarot and some of the other disciplines explored in this book could lead people to the gospel. Finally her daughter spoke. 'Mom, you don't get it. He's not coming for you, but coming for me.' Ross asked who 'me' was. She replied, 'I'm everything you describe. I've left mom's church and am exploring my own spirituality. Let's talk.'

> 'I see everything through a spiritual lens. I believe in a lot of astrology. I believe in aliens,' she said. 'I look up into the stars and I imagine: How self-important are we to think that we are the only life-form?' – Katy Perry
>
> Christina Garibaldi, 'Katy Perry Talks Boobs, Weed And Aliens' GQ *Magazine*, 2014

In this chapter, we are mindful that most followers of Jesus would believe that guidance aids like astrology and tarot are taboo. However, as we will explore, there are many within the church who are still interested or connected to these things. This may be because they are new to the faith and have had life experiences based on using such practices. Others of us have friends and family who are very much into these forms of guidance. The question is how does our conversation with them develop? As the chapter unfolds we consider the background, and there is more than meets the eye. Could tarot and astrology be 'preachers' of the 'unknown god'? Do they have a role in incarnational ministry among those who have an affinity with the 'spiritual but not religious' way of living? Also we will discuss that numerology, which may be connected to Feng Shui, turns up in daily commercial transactions.

The social surveys we referred to in the Introduction confirm that tools like tarot are widely used by those who identify with the 'spiritual but not religious'. Our experiences have also brought us in contact with many who believe these are very helpful tools for navigating their way through life.

BACKGROUND

The tarot card deck consists of 78 cards divided into two parts: the major arcana of 22 trumps and the minor arcana of 56 cards. Arcana is a term that refers to what is 'secret'. The origins of tarot have been the topic of much fanciful speculation, including claims that the cards came from Egypt as a pictorial work of deep wisdom. A careful investigation of the historical evidence does not support that claim. The earliest evidence is from Northern Italy in the 1400s where the cards were used to play a game called Triumphs. The pictures on the cards remind one of late medieval and early Renaissance culture.

Antoine Court de Gebelin was one of the first to claim that the tarot was a fortune-telling tool in late-eighteenth-century France. Another French occult thinker named Eliphas Levi (1810-1875) connected the tarot to the Cabala. Several sources influenced the painting of tarot imagery: the Bible, late medieval Catholic thought, Renaissance culture.

In recent decades practitioners link the tarot to Jung's theory of universal archetypes or symbols found in the human psyche that reflect universal needs for healing and renewal.[1] The major arcana are believed to contain those symbols that are primary for understanding the 'big picture' of life. Cards like 'death' and 'the tower,' are interpreted as referring to experiences that involve significant endings, and the visual symbols readily connect to archetypal figures like the 'Grim Reaper' or to catastrophes such as the Tower of Babel. The minor arcana, which are subdivided into four suits, covers the ordinary and 'lesser' parts of daily life. For example the 'three swords' pierce a heart that is surrounded by stormy clouds and such imagery links to an awareness of being symbolically pierced in body, mind and spirit. The cards connect with questions of guidance, issues of personality, relationships and vocation.

Today, a tarot reader operates in a counselling mode by listening to the client's story and then inviting them to shuffle the deck. Various cards are dealt and arranged to refer to aspects of life such as the recent, past, family relationships, work experiences, and immediate or near-future prospects. A reader will also observe a person's non-verbal bodily cues as the meaning of the cards is explored. Many readers we know see themselves as fulfilling the role once played by priests in the confessional. Astrology is a commonplace tool with an ancient pedigree reaching back to Mesopotamia, Egypt, Greece, Rome, Vedic and Chinese cultures. It was never a static tool in any of those cultures but developed as a means of interpreting celestial signs such as the movement of planets, constellations and the moon in conjunction with the seasons. It was used to forecast horoscopes for nations and kings, meteorological predictions, medical diagnosis, and predictive prophecies. In modern times, astrology has become a discipline for everyone to use in understanding self and others, connections with the divine, and decision-making.

> 'Astrology is basically about self-awareness ... It's about who you are and why you are here.'
> Barry Eaton, interviewed by Lenore Nicklin, 'Struck by the Stars,'
> *The Bulletin*, 29 September 1992, 45

Astrologers have always referred to the existence of the zodiac, which is an imaginary band or arc across the night sky. The sun appears to us on earth to move across that arc and there are twelve main constellations that likewise seem to follow the sun's movement. Month by month the constellation, that appears to rise first at night, changes and astrologers pinpoint the position of the sun, moon, and planets in relationship to that constellation. Each horoscope is subdivided into twelve houses through which the constellations and planets pass in the night sky. Each house influences different facets of life: personality, health, finance, relationships, career, worldview. The configuration of the constellation, and the place of the heavenly bodies, at the time of your birth is said to influence your personality.

The most important element in a horoscope is the Sun sign

which represents the Sun's position on the zodiac relative to the time of your birth. The sun sign refers to personality traits. The next in importance is called the rising sign. It refers to the angle of the rising of planets, moon and other bodies on the zodiac's arc. The rising sign refers to your character and traits. Horoscopes are used by astrologers to enable clients to explore life issues that were formerly the domain of counsellors and pastors.

In numerology it is claimed that our relationships, business ventures, personality and near-future decision-making may be interpreted by means of numbers. This is done by reducing to numbers one's name, birthday, and birthplace. Some believe that numerical patterns reveal the divine mind and such patterns can be found hidden in religious texts such as the Bible, Qur'an and Vedas. Other numerical patterns may be discerned in the structure of the cosmos and these things may be represented using numbers and letters of the alphabet. The classic understanding is that the universe has been constructed according to numerical patterns. The idea of numerical patterns is related to a concept of 'spiritual vibrations'. We experience vibrations within our bodies and we may detect similar vibrations in other objects. Numerologists insist that vibrations may be expressed mathematically and we look for the numerical patterns within or in other objects.

We are both associated with Morling Theological College which is building a residential university complex. This missional venture has obliged us to respond to Chinese numerology. Since most students are of Chinese ethnicity the architect and builder's question was whether there should be a floor numbered four because that is a number associated with bad luck and death.

Another architectural protocol was whether we would consider *Feng Shui*. The words Feng Shui refer to wind and water and their impact on the natural environment. In classic Chinese culture harmony is created in a building or a city by working out a good design that takes into account the forces of wind and water. A practitioner relies on a combination of ideas: the flow of cosmic/universal energy (Chi), the Taoist principles of Yin/Yang (two equal and opposite yet complementary forces), Chinese version of numerology and astrology and how these things impact on human well-being.

In order to design a good building a Feng Shui consultant will explore the links between the environment, the position of nearby trees, streams, hills and the stars and planets in the night sky. This is to ensure that Chi energy flows properly and our harmony with the natural environs will produce health, wealth and happiness. For example, a poor design will possibly cause a loss of wealth. It is believed that money will be lost where the front and back door are in a straight line. Creative designs that will ensure maximum harmony include hexagonal shaped windows, the placement of mirrors to reflect away bad energy and the position of furniture.

The design and use of spaces may be framed in a holistic fashion today. The taboo or to do question was the spirituality of Feng Shui going to be foundational to the building of the complex? It is a conversation that Christians involved in real estate and property development are facing today.

CONTACT POINTS

How many people today don't know their star-sign? How many don't take a peek at their daily horoscope in newspapers and magazines? However it is our experience that astrology in the west comes a 'poor' second after the tarot in terms of popularity and appeal. While many Christians reject tarot, astrology and numerology as having no place in the Christian's walk with Christ, it is important that we do not miss a critical pastoral point about conversion and discipleship. There are people who have become followers of Jesus but who may still retain elements of their pre-Christian faith, which might include reliance on tarot or astrology.

There is a helpful understanding that Dave Tomlinson pinpointed some years ago but which still remains true. Today, roughly 70% of those who have become followers of Jesus cannot recall a specific date for 'conversion'. Instead conversion for them has been a process. By way of contrast, Tomlinson noted that in times past 69% of Christians used to be able to cite a precise date for their conversion.[2] So, it is not surprising that many within churches today are in a process of figuring out what aspects of their life need to change and what will be discarded.

A recent example of this came when Philip was taking a seminar on alternative spirituality. During a short break, a woman in her thirties who was attending this church asked, 'What do you think about numerology?' Before Philip could even reply she began to tell her story. She was persuaded that God was speaking to her through numerology. Prior to becoming a follower of Jesus she had found guidance and direction in numerology, and had incorporated it as part of her new found faith. She explained that she was continually encountering the same number and believed that this was a sign from God. She interpreted the number as a sign that God wanted her to end her de facto relationship. Philip said that God could speak to us through all ways and means and even used a donkey to rebuke a prophet (Num. 22:22-35). Philip personally knew the pastoral team at the church was savvy enough to know when to offer her counsel on numerology. This is just one of many illustrations of the kinds of stories that many could recount from church life.

Outside the church context, contact points are everywhere from conversations with neighbours who are exploring spiritual disciplines, to the alternative new age bookshop and festival. Most people outside the church have interacted at some point with astrology and tarot. Numerology is surprisingly popular among many Muslims.

DISCERNMENT

Understandably Christians, whose ministry places strong emphasis on discerning heresy, and those who stress the spiritual warfare approach, will raise biblical concerns about tarot, astrology and numerology. A general pastoral warning is that the predictive aspects of astrology and tarot are unreliable and may put us in contact with harmful spiritual powers that are not from God. The warning points Christians to trust in God concerning their guidance and future. Their pastoral warnings and counsel deserve to be taken to heart. Most Christians would maintain that the Old Testament prohibits any interest in astrology and other tools of divination based on commands found in passages like Deut. 13:1-5; 18:9-14. A very direct rebuke against relying on astrology is:

> And beware lest you raise your eyes to heaven, and when you see the sun and the moon and the stars, all the host of heaven, you be drawn away and bow down to them and serve them, things that the Lord your God has allotted to all the peoples under the whole heaven. (Deut 4:19)

There are pointed commands that condemn certain divinatory practices. However, as some are quick to point out, the Bible does include 'divination'. For example, hydromancy (fleece reading) was actively used by God's people (e.g. Judges 6:37-40). Some notable characters were skilled in different divinatory techniques. Joseph had a cup of divination (Gen. 44:2-5) and interpreted dreams. Daniel also interpreted dreams (Dan. 2: 31-44; 4:19-27). The high priests of Israel used a form of stick or stone throwing divination using the Urim and Thummim (Deut. 33:8). The casting of lots was understood as one way of revealing God's will (Prov. 16:33). In the New Testament, Judas is replaced by Matthias through the casting of lots (Acts 1:26).

A lingering problem for modern-day Christians is the influence that nineteenth-century biblical scholarship has had in understanding divination's role across the ancient near east. It became an established view that the religion of Israel was typified by prophecy, while other ancient near eastern religions emphasised divination. In recent years that 'established' viewpoint has been discredited because (a) prophecy was not unique to Israel, and (b) Israel allowed some forms of divination as we have just noted. What has to be sorted out is the critical difference between the various types of divination and the important theological question, namely, 'which God are you dealing with?'[3] This is the question that is being asked in the scriptural narratives. In astrology one looks to the planets for guidance rather than the Creator of the planets. This is a vital concern that proponents of both the heresy and spiritual warfare models are correct in insisting is something that needs careful discussion.

However, what will arise in mission outreach settings is the question of whether there is a bridge that one may cross over from disciplines, such as tarot and astrology, to becoming a follower of Jesus?

This is not just a lively concern for say Christians living in India who daily interact with popular and village-life expressions of Hindu practice where the locals highly esteem astrology and numerology as tools for guidance. It will also hold true for Christians who interact with friends and the wider community where people respect tarot, astrology and numerology. Looking for 'bridges' is common in all missionary endeavours.

The issue for critical discernment will not just be about the 'heresies' associated with tarot, astrology and numerology. It will also include discerning, as Paul did in his use of quotes from the Stoic philosophers and poets in Athens (Acts 17:16-34), what contact points may allow us to creatively build a bridge to the gospel. In Paul's case he took lines from the poets that were not inconsistent with biblical faith but did not endorse or baptise everything that the Stoics said. He quoted them, 'In him we live and move and have our being ... for we are indeed his offspring' (Acts 17:28). Paul also linked the altar to an unknown god found in Athens to his storytelling of God as the creator of all life and to the resurrection of Jesus. When John Drane refers to the tarot as a possible 'altar to an unknown god' he says:

> Actually, the Tarot is by no means the only such 'altar' to be found in New Spirituality. Crystals, colours, healings, angels – all of these and more besides can become avenues for the invitation to follow Jesus. To identify these 'altars' we need to ask just one simple question in relation to any spiritual practice that we may find: does it focus attention on matters that are central to the gospel, even when the name of Christ is never mentioned?[4]

The bridge building is surprisingly quite straightforward when one considers the pictures on each tarot card. It is a bridge-building exercise without falling for the predictive element of the tarot but stimulates conversation on the big questions of life. The pictures may be linked up to the biblical story stretching from Genesis 1 to Revelation 22. A couple of quick illustrations may help to make this point clear. There is the Lovers card, which shows Adam and Eve in Eden: an angel hovers above them and beside them are two trees with a serpent curled around one tree. The card takes us immediately to the story of creation and fall in Genesis 2-3.The Devil card shows Adam and Eve in chains to the Devil, surrounded in complete blackness, symbolising their spiritual bondage.

The Hanged Man card shows a man with a halo around his head crucified upside down on a T-shaped cross. The wood of the cross bears life-giving leaves, which reminds us that in giving up his life Jesus gave new life to all who follow him. The Fool card is regarded by tarot experts as the key in the entire deck. It shows a man walking toward a precipice who seems unconcerned by the danger, followed by a faithful dog, and whose presence dispels all darkness in the world. In the eyes of the undiscerning Jesus appeared 'foolish' however, the New Testament declares that God's foolishness is wiser than human wisdom (1 Cor. 1:25; 4:10). Among serious practitioners of tarot the Fool is seen as a dying and rising deity. Joseph Campbell was a world specialist in myth whom George Lucas relied on in creating his mythic Star Wars characters. Campbell understood the Fool card as symbolizing the dying and resurrected sun god.[5]

The above is not 'forced' because it is very much a God-given bridge. The pictorial images are drawn from the Bible and were rooted in the Renaissance Christian world. One might anachronistically say the cards in that world were a 'power-point' illustration of God's redemptive story. We can move from Genesis to Revelation with the tarot deck. We did our homework on the origins and background of the tarot and in collaboration with Drane, set out the details in *Beyond Prediction*. We have applied the insights into the biblical meaning behind the cards in alternate spirituality festivals over many years. In another text Drane observes, 'Christians all over the world (including Britain) are now to be found with a positive presence in mind, body, spirit festivals – some of them using the Tarot, others offering something as simple as 'free prayer' – and people are coming to faith.'[6]

When Ross was in Ashville he took the students into a spiritual bookstore and wandered over to the section where the tarot decks were for sale. Ross picked up the classic Rider-Waite deck, which is widely honoured and respected by tarot users with a status akin to the King James Version of the Bible.

The store's owner asked Ross if he was a tarot reader. Ross said he looked for the deeper meaning of the cards from a Christian perspective. She asked him to explain this further. This chat occurred in public view. They then had a conversation about the Tolkien Lord of the Rings deck. She then indicated she had wanted to ask someone if Tolkien was a Christian. She thought that Ross was the 'sent' person. Ross replied that Tolkien was a Christian and they sat down over a coffee to talk more about Jesus and the cards.

If we participate in an Incarnational missional ministry we also need to appreciate that not everyone works in the same environments. For some there will also be the discernment principle about the weaker 'brother' and 'sister'. Some care and sensitivity is important for those who are younger in faith or for whom such matters are too close to their past journey and for whom these matters might cause one to stumble (1 Cor. 8:7-13). An alternative to the classic tarot deck is the Jesus deck which consists of four suits named after the four gospels, with illustrations from particular passages. This deck is free from all association with the Tarot. Both decks are visual and tell the gospel narrative.

In the case of astrology, when building bridges, a few points need to be kept clear. We have already mentioned the concerns about astrology. However, in our conversations what we may refer to are the intriguing biblical passages that mention the stars and even the zodiac. These biblical references may be used as a bridge to the gospel and the authenticity of the Bible. The Hebrew term for zodiac is Mazzaroth, and this is used in Job 38:33. The enigmatic Star of Jacob in Balaam's oracles (Num. 24:17) refers to a future ruler of Israel. Most commentators understand the passage as a messianic prophecy that links to Jesus' nativity.

There is also the relationship between Daniel and the Magi of Nebuchadnezzar's court and Daniel was promoted to be their chief (Dan. 2:48). The Magi were probably Persian astrologers and Zoroastrian priests. At the nativity of Jesus there were Magi who were guided by several things, including the heavenly star, angelic appearances in dreams, the scribes' knowledge of prophecies (Matt. 2:6), and presumably Daniel's predictions about the messiah-king (Dan. 9). The lesson here is that the Magi, as astrologers, meet Christ the creator of the cosmos. Here is a bridge for those who are interested in astrology.

Another point relates to church history. There will be instances where a conversation partner knows that the Christian response to astrology has not always involved a wholesale rejection of it. They may want to justify astrology from the 'forgotten' Christian heritage.

There are actually three historically based Christian responses: rejection, qualified acceptance, apologetic engagement.

Some early Church Fathers, such as Hippolytus and Augustine, rejected astrology because of its links to planetolatry (worshipping the planets as deities), and the belief in cosmic determinism (everything is predetermined and ruled by the heavenly bodies). The church of the modern era has rightly expressed concerns that astrology is idolatrous and involves divination by relying on planets and stars. It has also tended to reject astrology because it is unscientific.

Other church fathers who rejected astrology for its determinism nevertheless saw some positive contact points. Clement of Alexandria and John Chrysostom agreed that the Magi were Persians who came to Christ. Bishop Zeno of Verona composed a baptismal sermon where he Christianised the meaning of the zodiac and explained that anyone who is born again has a brand new 'star-sign' in Christ Jesus.

> 'Luther was not keen on astrology and remarked on one occasion that his friend and disciple Melanchthon pursued astrology, 'as I take a drink of strong beer when I am troubled with grievous thoughts.'
>
> John Warwick Montgomery, *Principalities and Powers*
> (Minneapolis: Bethany, 1975), 65.

Keen followers of astrology know that during the Reformation prominent Lutherans, such as Melanchthon, Chemnitz, Brahe and Kepler, were all students of astrology. Melanchthon cast horoscopes in the belief that the creation is God's book of nature and that it confirms biblical truth. In Melanchthon's day the dividing line between astrology and astronomy was not very clear. The Lutherans rejected predictive and deterministic astrology but they were open to understanding the possible influence of the moon, sun and planets on the weather. John Calvin believed that planetary bodies could influence our body in medical diagnosis.

The third response of apologetic engagement is an attempt to show that the zodiac signs point to the message of the gospel. The gospel in the stars approach suggests that the twelve constellations symbolically refer to key biblical themes or events, such as Virgo points to the Virgin Birth of Christ. It is claimed that the name of one of the stars in this constellation literally means 'the seed', and so we have the Virgin and child of biblical prophecy also symbolised in the zodiac. The possibility that the cosmos, and specifically the stars, point us to God is affirmed in the Bible (Rom. 10:18; Ps. 19):

> The heavens declare the glory of God, and the sky above proclaims his handiwork ... Their voice goes out through all the earth, and their words to the end of the world. (Ps. 19:1 & 4)

The gospel in the stars is a highly speculative theory and claims about it being a heavenly foretelling of the gospel drama may be prone to exaggeration. However, it is worth noting that even with those reservations being understood, the gospel in the stars has been used in a positive way in conversations in alternate spirituality festivals.[7] For those who are involved in Incarnational ministry or faith-sharing they will acknowledge the concerns about predictive astrology while also having their eyes open for the creative opportunities to build bridges.

Numerology is problematic because of its determinist view of life: your personality, relationships and direction in life are established by numerical patterns. Numerical patterns may seem fascinating but they do not constitute proof of any cause-and-effect relationships between us and the rest of the universe.

However, we must be careful not to be completely dismissive about the symbolic importance of numbers when we read through the Bible. There are some significant numbers such as 666, the number of man, seven for the week of creation, twelve for the patriarchal tribes and number of original apostles, forty days (Jesus in the wilderness) or years (Israel's wandering).

Understandably, many will feel the need to contrast these practices with Christian faith, and to teach accordingly for equipping and discipleship. The question of taboo or to do will be more directed to our approach to Incarnational ministry.

CASE STUDIES

We know of Bible study groups and colleges that are interested in creative outreach and have trained participants in how to build bridges to the gospel from the tarot. Here is an interesting example of how this sort of training may bear fruit in a family context. A college student had attended a Bible college class where the bridge building from the tarot pictures to the gospel was explained. After the class he returned home and walked into a family argument. His parents were devout Christians and they were upset. His sister, who was living away from home as a university student, had dropped in for a visit. She told her parents that she no longer felt any connection to Christianity. Instead, she was exploring tarot cards and other aspects of alternate spiritualities. Her parents walked out of the room feeling angry and distressed by her spiritual choices. Her brother did not react negatively. For him here was a God-given moment to apply what he had just studied that afternoon. He took her interest in tarot as an opportunity to show that he understood why she felt drawn to the cards. He suggested that she might find it interesting to take a fresh look at the tarot cards and their link to the Bible's message. They looked at the pictures on the major arcana cards, and he was able to illustrate the essentials of the apostolic faith.

For those who enter into Incarnational ministries, there are times when doors open to sharing. For example, Philip was invited to speak at a world conference of tarot practitioners about our book, *Beyond Prediction*, and had an hour to outline the biblical story of the gospel through the tarot cards.

A creative avenue for Incarnational ministry is participating as an exhibitor in alternate spirituality festivals and fairs. In 'Starting the Conversation' chapter we share how such festivals are not difficult to enter. In the 1990s we co-founded the Community of Hope that reached into Mind*Body*Spirit festivals in Australia and elsewhere. In England we are mindful of the work of Sanctus1 that had exhibitor's booths in festivals.[8]

As well they have conducted the Spirit of Life Christian spirituality fair in Coventry Cathedral. This once bombed but majestically rebuilt Cathedral naturally draws people from a variety of spiritual interests and backgrounds. The fair had five objectives that are transferable to other such contexts:

- To be a 'spiritual fair' with a wide variety of activities
- To explore the spiritual realm
- To be open to anyone and everyone
- To be planned in consultation with the churches in Coventry to relate to and hopefully
- To assist them in their mission to their city.

In entering a ministry in a festival the basic thing is that the booth needs to be attractively decorated and well planned. This is normally worked out by visiting the festival and carefully noting how it operates and the structure of other booths. With respect to using the tarot as outlined above, one may erect a table and chairs from which valuable interpersonal conversations may unfold on the deeper meaning of the tarot card images. The details on the meaning of each tarot card are explained in *Beyond Prediction* and it also includes illustrated exercises on how to present the gospel via tarot.

Here is a brief real-life encounter that simply demonstrates how a conversation may develop:

> Sharon and I discussed for some time how the cards mimic archetypes and symbols that reveal our common search for meaning. I specifically asked Sharon if she was aware of the message of the resurrection in the cards. I explained the Judgment card (card XX) is full of hope and life in its apocalyptic symbolism. Attached to the angel's trumpet is a pennant which features a red cross, the universal symbol of healing. Sharon noticed in the foreground of the card that people are rising from their graves in joy, and I pointed out the contrast with the Death card (card XIII) where the people have succumbed to the agent of death. I said, 'Sharon, the image on the card is one of resurrection, not reincarnation. The cards testify to a universal resurrection hope.' At Sharon's request I then gave a 'reading' of the cards that covered our universal bliss as seen in the Lovers' card, our fall (Death and Tower card), our universal search for transformation (Hermit card) and the one who restores the Lovers' Utopia (Fool card). I shared with Sharon that Jesus did not remain dead. The Chariot card (card VII) signifies that he arose triumphantly and shattered the hold of death forever, a shattering that the Judgment card illustrates awaits all those who know and love his name.[9]

ASTROLOGY, TAROT AND NUMEROLOGY

In a similar fashion, an exhibitor's booth may be decorated around a theme that links the classic Zodiac signs of the constellations with the gospel message. A booth may be designed to prompt conversations and questions. Our experience highlights that a good interactive booth will:

> Have visual displays of the zodiacal signs with a 'mystical' appearance of Christ at the centre intimating his supremacy over everything.
>
> Use the biblical Magi episode (Matt. 2) as a conversation point between the visitor's quest for meaning and the gospel story. This could be reinforced by a pamphlet that covers the topic. An important point that should emerge in a conversation is that even ancient astrologers recognised Christ's supremacy and their response was to worship him.
>
> Use the visual arts in pictures and/or music to represent the praise of creation (e.g. Psalm 19). It helps to connect creation's praise with our common feeling of awe at the magnificence of the creation. Conversations may cover becoming aware of creation's witness to God.
>
> Offer a prayer-chair where a visitor may feel moved to express their need for guidance and closer contact with God.
>
> Offer a post-festival interactive seminar where people who have expressed interest might gather for a deeper group discussion about the zodiacal signs as possible pointers to Christ.

In the case of numerology we observed an exhibitor's booth that invited visitors to discover the root meaning of their forename. The basis for doing this is that in both Hebrew and Greek the alphabetical letters also have numerical values. The process involved tallying up the numerical value of their name and then talking about the biblical meaning for particular numbers. For individuals whose forename actually comes from the Bible, such as Sarah and John, it was possible to talk further about the significance of that name.

THINGS TO DO

As a church or group survey your friends, family, and neighbours to see whether they are open to astrology, tarot, or numerology. If so, is it a bit of 'fun' or does it involve a deeper spiritual connection? Ask if you can pray with them for direction and guidance.

START THE CONVERSATION

1. In your group share whether tarot or astrology has been part of your journey. Share whether you would be comfortable with the bridge building missional opportunities.
2. Charles Kraft, missiologist at Fuller Seminary and leader in spiritual warfare, advised us that he would use the tarot cards as we have outlined but only after he had prayed over the cards to remove any undue spiritual influences or possible harm. Discuss what you think about Kraft's insight.
3. Read Psalm 19 and share in your group about the vastness of God's creation.

9
CHRISTIAN BLESSINGS FOR PETS –
Honouring creation or frivolous fluff?[1]

The Vicar of Dibley is a classic English TV comedy. In one episode the Revd Geraldine Granger (Dawn French) decides to conduct a service for blessing animals. David Horton (Gary Waldhorn), an influential member of the parish council, pooh-poohed the idea. He asked if she was 'bollocking crazy' and afterwards he complained to the bishop. Geraldine was warned that she could lose her parish appointment and things worsened when a tabloid newspaper ridiculed the proposed service.

Geraldine was pleasantly surprised when a good crowd accompanied by sheep, cows, horses, goats, hens, rabbits, dogs and other animals, gathered for the service. She greeted a skinhead who came with his spaniel named 'Satan'. David had a change of heart and realised that the service was wonderful.[2] More than twenty years have elapsed since the episode was originally broadcast and its pop cultural reputation endures. England's *Daily Echo* carried this pre-Christmas headline in December 2014, 'Church hosts Vicar of Dibley-style carol service for animals'.[3] The minister at St Ambrose Anglican Church in Bournemouth felt that Christmas was an appropriate time to give thanks to God for pets because nativity scenes of Jesus' birth have traditionally included the donkey and ox (cf. Isa. 1:3).

> ### REFLECTION
>
> 'In the coming reign of God, we will not leave behind the coral reefs, the hummingbirds, the cold-water algae of the Antarctic, or the countless species now extinct ... If the Resurrection of Jesus and the experiences of the disciples between Easter and Pentecost is an indication of what lies in store for the universe then the future will be a transformation of the laws of nature as we now know them into something so transcendently joyous that weeping and pain and disease and dying will be nevermore, and 'the lion will lay down with the lamb' ... Somehow all of nature, and not just humankind, is destined to eternal life with God in community with each other, a community of unending and bliss-filled experience.'
>
> Robert John Russell, 'Five Attitudes Toward Nature and Technology From a Christian Perspective,' *Theology and Science* 1 (2003): 156-157.

In Auckland New Zealand the October 4, 2015 Global March for World Animal Day became the focal point for 'blessing of the animals'. The festivity brought together Auckland's Society for the Prevention of Cruelty to Animals (SPCA), St Matthew-in-the-city Anglican church, the City Council, Police, and the Heaven Bent Gospel Choir. It began with brunch in Albert Park and a procession of pets walked to church. There was a musical proclamation about God's creatures, followed by *Amazing Grace* and the call to worship. The SPCA chairman lit a remembrance candle for pets that have died while another officer read Bible passages. There was a sermon, prayers, the Gospel choir performed and the congregation sang classic hymns about animals. In the ritual blessing three Anglican clergy officiated along with a Tibetan Buddhist monk.[4]

On the same day a low-key service was celebrated at St Mark's Anglican Church in the Sydney suburb of South Hurstville. The evangelical minister the Revd Peter Greenwood officiated with liturgical prayers, classic hymns and a short gospel lesson. Since

2007 when the service began irregular churchgoers have brought lizards, rabbits, goldfish, hens, cats and dogs for blessing.

Church services for blessing pets are popular across the USA. St John the Divine Episcopal (Anglican) Cathedral in New York City has hosted pet services for thirty years.[5] Six thousand people attended the Cathedral's 1989 service and YouTube has clips of recent services.[6] In 2015 pet services were held in twenty-one Episcopal churches in Louisiana including New Orleans Cathedral.[7] St James Lutheran Church (Michigan) and Grace Lutheran Church (North Carolina) have held blessing services for several years.[8] The United Methodist churches' track-record goes back to 1992.[9] Brent Beasley, who is the senior pastor at Broadway Baptist Church in Fort Worth Texas, has officiated at pet services for eight years.[10] The Central Christian Church (Disciples of Christ) in Dallas has a successful community outreach through its service.[11]

Christians are polarised between those who rejoice and those who reject pet services. Supporters believe pet services bear witness to God's love for all creatures and remind us that God holds us accountable for maltreating animals. Some question pet services feeling that the church has been infiltrated by Pagan and/or secular influences. We are often asked if this is true and, don't these services take our focus off the gospel? Isn't this taboo?

BACKGROUND

Four sources led to the creation of pet services in the last quarter of the twentieth century:

- The Bible.
- Church narratives, liturgies, art and architecture for blessing animals.
- RSPCA and 'Animal Sunday' services.
- The reinvention of St Francis of Assisi as the patron saint of ecology and animals.

BIBLICAL TOPICS AND ANIMALS

Anti-Cruelty: Positive models: Rebekah and camels (Gen. 24:12-48), Jacob's flocks (Gen. 33: 13-14); Law and wisdom: (Deut. 22:10; 25:4; Exod. 23:12; Lev. 25:6-7; Prov. 12:10). Cruel cases: Simeon and Levi (Gen 49:6); Balaam (Num. 22:22-35); Samson (Judges 14:5-6; 15:4-5).

Atonement: Sacrificial offerings (Abraham in Gen 15:8-11 & 22:9-13, Passover in Exod. 12, the Tabernacle and Temple; abrogated by the Cross Heb. 9-10).

Blessing and Creation Covenant: Gen.1:20-25; 8:15-19; 9:9-17; Hos. 2:18.

Diet (OT): All creatures were intended to be vegetarian (Gen. 1:29-30). Flesh-eating is tolerated as a concession to our sinful hearts (Gen. 9:2-4); Isaac's appetite for luxurious meat leads to his undoing (Gen. 27:2-38; cf. Prov. 15:17; 23:1-3, 6). Israel's ideal diet was meatless (Deut. 8:7-10; Jer. 29:5; Amos 9:14). 'Clean/Unclean' animals and diet linked to purity (Lev. 11; Deut. 14:3-20).

Future Earth: Creatures reconciled (Isa. 11:6-9; 43:20; 65:17-25; Hos. 2:18; Zech. 2:4; Rom. 8:19-22; 1 Cor. 15: 27-28; Eph. 1:10; Col. 1:15-20; Rev. 21:5).

Idolatry: Animals misused for false worship (Exod. 32; Rom. 1:23) and animal sacrifices from the unrepentant were rejected (1 Sam. 13:8-13; Jer. 6:20; Amos 5:21-22).

Judgment: Animals act as instruments of judgment (Exod. 8 & 10; 1 Kings 13: 23-25; 2 Kings 2:23-24; Joel 1:4; Rev. 19:17-18).

Praise: Animals praise God (Ps. 65:12-13; 69:34; 96:11-12; 98:7-8; 103:22; 145:10; 148; 150:6; 1 Chron.16:31-32; Isa. 43:20; 44:23; 55:12; Rev. 5:13).

Prophecy: Peaceful kingdom (Isa. 11:6-9; 34:14-17; 65:25; Zech. 2:4; 14:20). The coming king rides a donkey (Zech. 9:9).

Providence: God provides for animals (Ps. 104:17-30; Job 38-41; Gen.9:9-17; Joel 2:22; Matt. 10:29; Luke 12:6-7, 24).

Redemption: God saves both humans and beasts (Gen. 6:19-7:16; Ps. 36:6; Jonah 3:7-8; 4:11). Like Noah's Ark, animals and people are rescued from polytheistic Egypt (Gen. 12:16; Exod. 12:31-32, 38).

Bible

English theologian Colin Brown wrote 'it has been estimated that animals are mentioned some 3,000 times in the Bible'.[12] Philip tested that claim and counted 2,853 references for insects, birds, domesticated, wild and sea creatures in *Young's Analytical Concordance to the Bible.*

Many biblical stories feature animals: Creation (Gen. 1-2), Noah (Gen. 6-9), Balaam's donkey (Num. 22: 22-35), David the shepherd (1 Sam. 17:34-37), Nathan's parable of the lamb (2 Sam. 12:1-6), Elijah and the ravens (1 Kings 17:6) and fiery horse-drawn chariot (2 King 2:11-12), Jonah (1:17-2:10; 3:7; 4:11), Daniel and lions (Dan. 6). Jesus taught that God cares for birds (Matt. 10:29; Luke 12:6-7, 24). He fulfilled Zechariah's prophecy (9:9) of riding a donkey on Palm Sunday (Matt. 21:1-10). Christ rides a white horse to victory (Rev. 19:11-16).

God's creatures

Animals actually reflect God's glory and wisdom (Ps.104:14-15; Prov. 6:6), know and obey God (Ps. 104:27-30; Job 12:7-11; Joel 1:20; 2:22; Isa. 1:3; 43:20; Jonah 1:17) and recognise angels (Num. 22:22-27). Every creature belongs to God (Ps.24; 50:10-11; 65:5-13; 66:1-4; 89:11; 96:5-13; 104; 145:8-13).

Vocation to Bless

Pet services build on the fact that God blesses all creatures on the first page of the Bible (Gen. 1:20-25). The blessing is repeated after the Flood (Gen. 8:15-19) and supports God's promised peace for creatures (Hos. 2:18; Isaiah 11:6-9; 43:20; 65:17-25; Zech. 2:4). God chose humans to be co-workers with him in the blessing (Gen. 1:26-2:24; Ps. 8). Emerging church author Scott Bader-Saye says that Adam's vocation for blessing animals is assigned to us.[13]

God enjoys a direct relationship with every living creature (Gen. 1-2; Job 38-41; Ps.104:1-25). Birds that nested in the temple's eaves were blessed (Ps. 84:3-4). Rabbis in biblical times taught that as we bless the creation we are blessing God.[14] William Dumbrell indicates that God's post-Flood covenant with creation and animals is crucial (Gen. 9: 9-17).[15] Martin Luther commented:

> Careful note must be taken of the phrase 'for all future generations,' for it includes not only the human beings of that time and the animals of that time but all their offspring until the end of the world.[16]

The prophets' message about blessing is clear: the prosperity of the land and animals is interwoven with the flourishing of God's people (Hos. 2:18; Joel 2:22; Isa. 11:6-9; 43:20; 65:25; Zech. 2:4).[17] Israel's disobedience brings suffering to all creatures and the land (e.g. Deut. 28; Joel 1).

A key theme for blessing animals is Noah's righteousness (Gen. 6:9; 7:1). The rabbis taught that righteousness went hand-in-glove with caring for God's creatures:

> Two men were called righteous because they fed the creatures of the Holy One, blessed be He. They were Noah and Joseph.[18]

In a world that spiralled out of control (Gen 6:12-13) Noah's righteousness sharply contrasted with the debauchery, violence and cruelty to animals practiced at that time. Ruth Padilla DeBorst is a Latin American evangelical who believes that the post-Flood covenant mandates *here and now* that we enter into righteous relationships with all creatures and the whole earth.[19]

Blessing pets is further linked to Christ's redemptive work and the resurrection hope of dwelling on a new earth (cf. 1 Cor. 15: 27-28; Col. 1:15-20; Eph. 1:10; Rev. 21:5; 2 Pet. 3:13).[20] John Gibbs' study of Paul's theology of creation and redemption included a careful analysis of the Greek word *Ktsis* (translated as 'creation' or 'creature') in Rom. 8:19-22. He concluded that all creation will be transformed.[21] Colin Kruse comments: 'Paul makes it clear that God's redemptive work not only restores the lost glory of human beings ... but also involves the renewal of the whole creation.'[22]

> **ROMANS 8:19-22**
>
> For the creation waits with eager longing for the revealing of the sons of God. For the creation was subjected to futility, not willingly, but because of him who subjected it, in hope that the creation itself will be set free from its bondage to corruption and obtain the freedom of the glory of the children of God. For we know that the whole creation has been groaning together in the pains of childbirth until now.

Church Narratives, Liturgy, Art and Architecture

Early church leaders Papias, Irenaeus, Methodius and Theophilus of Antioch believed on the basis of Rom. 8:19-22 and Isaiah's prophecy that animals will live in a new Eden.[23] Frescoes on church pavements excavated in Antioch and elsewhere show animals living in harmony.[24] This contrasted with the Roman gladiatorial blood-sports where Christians were martyred and wild animals were slaughtered on such a massive scale that some European and North African species became extinct.

Some medieval Christians believed that animals are included

in creation's future destiny. Stories about saints and wild animals living in peace gave glimpses of eternity.[25] However, many medieval theologians denied this future destiny based on two things: (a) a reinterpretation of Rom. 8:19-22; (b) differences between human and animal souls.

Eden's future was reimagined without plants and animals because it was believed that they are temporary things for our use and we won't need them in eternity.[26] The 'creature' in Rom. 8:19-22 was reinterpreted as referring to angels or unrepentant people or inanimate objects. This reimagining has sadly influenced the contemporary church.

A long-winded debate from the fifth to the seventeenth century contrasted the 'perishable souls' of animals with 'rational souls' of humans.[27] Thomas Aquinas (1224-1274) argued that only a 'rational soul' may be resurrected. Greek philosophical ideas about rational souls shaped the interpretation of biblical passages concerning God's image in humans (Gen. 1:26-27).[28]

From Reformation to C. S. Lewis
Martin Bucer (1491-1551) became a Protestant reformer after hearing Luther talk in 1518. In *Instruction in Christian Love* (1523) Bucer argued from Rom 8:19-22 and other passages that animals will be resurrected. He elaborated his view in a commentary on Romans (1536) and refuted Aquinas' argument about no future destiny for animals. John Calvin (1509-1564) who studied under Bucer believed that creation's renewal includes animals.[29] the Revd John Bradford (1510-1555) was mentored by Bucer and martyred in Mary Tudor's reign however before he was executed Bradford wrote a swansong letter explaining that animals will be resurrected and quoted Bucer.[30]

The apologists Bishop Butler (1692-1752) and Richard Dean (1726-1778) affirmed the resurrection of animals.[31] John Wesley (1703-1791) preached 'The Great Deliverance' based on Rom. 8:19-22 arguing for the resurrection of animals.[32] Wesley opposed vivisection (experiments on animals) and was a vegetarian. Many would not know that he and his brother

Charles wrote hymns with verses of animals praising God that have been deleted in modern hymn-books. In a pub debate Augustus Montague Toplady (1740-1778), who wrote the hymn *Rock of Ages*, opposed cruelty to animals and affirmed their resurrection.[33]

C. S. Lewis looked after many pets and opposed vivisection in his novel *That Hideous Strength*. The Narnia stories feature non-human creatures joining the child heroes under the leadership of Aslan the Lion (a Christ figure). Lewis accepted the Psalmist's witness that animals praise God and he thought that some pets might be included in the afterlife.[34]

'APOSTLES' AND ANIMALS

Apocryphal texts recount stories: Peter enables a dog to talk, and resurrects from the dead a salt-sea fish (Acts of Peter); Thomas blesses a talking donkey (Acts of Thomas), and wild animals refuse to kill Thecla when the Romans order her death (Acts of Paul and Thecla). The historical evidence for these stories is weak but suggests an animal-friendly early church.

'In the writings of John Cassian ... there is a charming tradition about the apostle John in his later years at Ephesus. One day while the aged saint was gently stroking a pet partridge, a young man who had just come in from hunting, said, 'I'm surprised to see an illustrious man like you doing something so unimportant.' To which the apostle replied, 'What's that in your hand?' 'My bow,' said the hunter. 'Well,' John continued, 'if it was always bent, it would lose its elasticity and power. So I need this relief for my mind lest it lose its spring.'

Frank E. Gaebelein, *The Christian, The Arts, And Truth: Regaining The Vision of Greatness*, ed. D. Bruce Lockerbie (Portland, Oregon: Multnomah, 1985), 254-255.

Art, Architecture and Ark

An old joke is that the Church is just like Noah's Ark: if it wasn't for the storm outside you wouldn't tolerate the stench inside! The early church met in the catacombs which they decorated by painting biblical stories. The most frequently painted stories were Noah's Ark, Jonah and the sea creature, and Daniel among lions not only as reminders of God's deliverance but also as signs of the resurrection.[35] Several painted animals symbolised Christ's resurrection: dolphin, eagle, lion, panther, peacock, pelican.

Early church fathers such as Justin Martyr, Cyprian and Tertullian, likened the Church to the Ark as a place of salvation. Noah's Ark inspired the building of places of worship. At Mopsuestia in Turkey, a fourth-century church was excavated with a mosaic of Noah's Ark that only features animals which was inscribed 'The saving Ark of Noah'.[36] Adreina Contessa noted in her study of medieval Spanish art:

> Since very early times, Noah's Ark with all its inhabitants was synonymous with the Church, saving the seed of all forms of life.[37]

ORTHODOX CHURCHES

'The nave of the church ... symbolizes the transfigured creation, the new earth and the new heavens, and at the same time, the Church ... A church is, therefore, the prefiguration of the peace to come, of the new heavens, and of the new earth where all creatures will gather around their Creator.'

Leonid Ouspensky, *Theology of the Icon*, Vol. 1 (Crestwood, New York: St Vladimir's Seminary Press, 1992), 28 & 30.

In churches the congregation sit in the nave (Latin word 'navis' for ship) which symbolises a voyage:

The church proper was usually a rectangle, known as the body or nave. The very name indicates the symbolical conception. The church was conceived as a ship under full sail, riding forward to heaven and eternity.[38]

Liturgy
Dom Ambrose Agius explains that Catholic liturgy includes the blessing of animals:

> It is strange that Catholics should ever be surprised and even offended by public blessings of animals, organised by the Church. Actually, such blessings are as old as the Liturgy. Some of them, as a public ritual and indeed festival, go back a long way, like those in Rome on St Anthony's Day and in Latin America.[39]

Roman Catholic services for blessing animals are normally scheduled for January 17 which is the feast of St Anthony the Abbott (251-356). St Anthony was one of the early desert fathers renowned for living peacefully with wild animals. Catholic services for blessing animals are very popular in Italy, Spain, Peru and Mexico and although a century ago Peruvian Catholics blessed animals on All Souls' Day, they now celebrate it on St Francis' day (October 4).[40]

Eastern Orthodox liturgies include prayers for the blessing and protection of animals. A Russian Orthodox prayer for animals may be read at the Feast of St Mamas (September 2) who lived in the third century and icons portray him riding a lion. Greek Orthodox churches honour St Modestos, the protector and healer of animals (December 16), with a prayer for blessing animals. Prayers during Christmas, Epiphany, Lent and Easter week include animals as praise-partners and witnesses to Jesus' life.

Ethiopian Church
Abune Gäbrä Mänfäs Qeddus is Ethiopia's greatest saint and icons depict lions and leopards lying next to him. Aksum is the spiritual home for the Ethiopian Orthodox Tewahedo Church where stands the Church of the Four Animals. Every November a festival

celebrates God placing the four living creatures near his throne (Rev. 4:6-11; 5:11-12). Each one has facial features resembling a man, lion, ox and eagle. Ethiopians believe the man prays for humans, the lion prays for land animals, the ox prays for cattle and the eagle prays for birds.[41] The liturgy closes with these words: 'Salutation to the Four Beasts and to the horses of the Cherubim.'[42]

FOUR LIVING CREATURES

'In my view the living creatures themselves are certainly heavenly creatures, superior to all earthly creatures, as we have noted in connexion with their eyes and wings. But they are representatives of the world of earthly creatures in the sense that they worship on behalf of the latter. They act as priests of creation, offering continuous praise to God in the heavenly sanctuary on behalf of all creatures.'

Richard Bauckham, *Living With Other Creatures: Green Exegesis and Theology* (Waco: Baylor University Press, 2011), 177..

RSPCA and Animal Sunday

In early modern England it was considered 'manly' behaviour to torment animals in hunting, bull-baiting and dog-fights. On Shrove Tuesday (the day before Lent) it was customary for crowds to kill roosters by throwing sticks or stones at them. England earned the tag 'hell for horses' because horses, donkeys and dogs were abused until they dropped dead while hauling carriages.[43]

The publishing of anti-cruelty sermons became very 'popular from the 1820s onwards'.[44] It coincided with the creation of the Society for the Prevention of Cruelty to Animals which was the brainchild of the Revd Arthur Broome (1789-1837). Broome was an Anglican evangelical who ministered in London's East End and believed in the resurrection of animals.[45] Broome invited over two dozen social reformers, including the evangelical anti-slave campaigners Thomas Fowell Buxton (1786-1845) and William Wilberforce (1759-1833), to a coffee house where on June 16, 1824, they founded the SPCA. Broome served as founding secretary (1824-1828), personally paid the salary for an inspector and published anti-cruelty literature. It became the RSPCA in 1840 when Queen Victoria became its patron. Christian social reformers created 'cousin' SPCA groups in Australia, Canada, New Zealand and USA.

The forerunner to pet services is 'Animal Sunday' which began in London on July 9, 1865 when Arthur Penryhn Stanley (1815-1881), the Dean of Westminster, preached a sermon on behalf of the RSPCA.[46] The idea was to encourage churches to support the RSPCA by preaching annually against cruelty to animals. The services did not involve pets brought to church for blessings.

Animal Sunday services took root in Australia in the 1890s.[47] Tasmania's SPCA noted in 1909 that 'more sermons on the subject were preached last year, some of the clergy responding heartily to the request'.[48] In 1905 the SPCA invited New Zealand's churches to introduce Animal Sunday but the clergy were generally apathetic.[49] The SPCA persisted until in 1908 the *Wanganui Chronicle* reported that 'Animal Sunday is to be a different sort of day' because the churches were teaching the importance of kindness to God's creatures.[50] The Revd Algernon Colvile (1861-1918) assumed a leading role in Auckland with his sermons published annually in the newspaper.[51]

Animal Sunday services were still celebrated in South Australia in 1945 but church enthusiasm gradually declined in England, New Zealand and across Australia.[52] In the 1930s the RSPCA in these three nations began promoting 'animal welfare week' among the community generally.[53] Secular thinkers gradually assumed moral leadership on animal issues and, at a 1931 ecological conference, October 4 was dubbed World Animal Day.[54]

St Francis of Assisi
In 1979 Pope John Paul II declared St Francis of Assisi the patron saint of ecology and he was in some respects animal-friendly.

However over the past century St Francis has been mythically reinvented by lots of writers.[55] St Francis' feast day was settled on as October 4 which coincides with World Animal Day. American Episcopalian and Protestant churches began holding pet blessing services on St Francis' day not long after the Pope's declaration.

CONTACT POINTS

Pets and other animals are found in so many areas of our lives, among our neighbours, vet hospitals, farms, zoos, and animal shelters. There are so many animal charities of which the RSPCA is the world's oldest running.

DISCERNMENT

We form close bonds with our pets and responsible pet ownership is one way of enjoying God's gift of life (Ps. 115:15-16). Yet when is the last time you heard a sermon or talk on pets and the kingdom of God?

Pet ownership is rarely discussed by the community of faith but it does raise many ethical issues. Billions of dollars are extravagantly spent on pets while many people starve. Simultaneously thousands of pets are discarded annually at animal shelters. Responsible pet breeders are under-cut by unlicensed breeders raising puppies and kittens in squalid conditions. Companion animals are deliberately injured in many cases of domestic violence and elder abuse.

Ethical and theological concerns about animals extend beyond how we treat pets. Criminal enterprises poach birds, reptiles and endangered species. Safari tourism advertises wild animals slaughtered as trophies.[56] Some corporations test chemical products on animals as a safeguard against future law-suits over poor warning labels. Enormous profits generated by the fast-food industry rely on the mass production of genetically engineered farm animals that often live in squalid conditions.

Credible estimates are that a billion birds die annually across Canada and the USA due to collisions with reflective windows on skyscrapers.[57] Wildlife habitats are shrinking in Latin America as land is cleared to harvest crops to supply the US bio-fuel industry. The 2010 Gulf of Mexico oil disaster and the repetitive oil leaks in West Africa's Niger Delta are two examples of industrial ventures damaging aquatic habitats.[58]

A SOBER WARNING

'The Christian teacher must either drop the claim that the religion he advocates is the ultimate in 'goodness', or else he must somehow fit into his doctrine the duty of the Christian to protect the subhuman creatures of this planet from unscrupulous human acts now that we know that animals not only have nervous systems, but that some of them have nervous systems which are in certain details more highly developed than our own. If the Christian preacher fails to make the necessary adjustment, in the very near future he is going to find himself teaching something which thousands of Christians, non-Christians, atheists, anti-Christians and materialists will instinctively sense as unsatisfactory, and he will certainly not be helping to establish the claim made by Jesus that He is the Son of God.'

Charles D. Niven, *History of the Humane Movement*
(New York: Transatlantic Arts, 1967), 23-24.

Christian lawyers may make an educational and legal mark now that more than a hundred law schools across the USA, England, Australia and New Zealand teach 'animal law'. Sadly both legal textbooks and mass-market books on animal protection issues present a narrative that typecasts Christianity as a chauvinist religion discriminating against animals ('speciesism').[59] This hostile interpretation stems from anti-Christian books by nineteenth-century authors Edward Payson Evans and Henry Salt. Peter Singer, Lynn White and others have further refined the narrative. Rod Preece, a political scientist who has had a long association with Canada's SPCA, comments on the distortion of history:

> The disconcerting reality is that the academic field of animals and civilization is strewn with holier than history attitudes whereby all was dark and dismal until our modern-day heroes strode onto the field of honour and announced for the first time the rights of animals and our obligatory respect for them ... Proclaiming heroes and villains becomes the quest rather than understanding the complexities of past realities.[60]

Christians who are challenged to sift through the issue to accept or reject pet services must reflect on their motives and message. Many will not be comfortable with inter-faith blessing services such as occurred in Auckland. Some conservative Protestants have misgivings because of the connection made to St Francis of Assisi. Of course a pet blessing service does not have to operate along inter-faith lines or celebrate St Francis. Churches that celebrate pet blessings must ensure that they are doing so for the right reason, namely that animals matter to God. Non-Christians are quick to discern that a gathering is not genuine when animals are used as a gimmick to draw a crowd.

Churches that decide against pet blessings should find ways to bear witness to the full range of biblical truth about animals. Broome and Wilberforce challenged cruel values in their time. Charles Spurgeon was very vocal in sermons and articles about condemning animal cruelty as sin. Rev. Tony Sargent, who served at the evangelical Worthing Tabernacle (Sussex), launched a public protest campaign in the early 1990s against England's live export trade.[61]

Philip Sampson is an evangelical ethicist and a Fellow of the Oxford Centre for Animal Ethics. He recently pointed out that many younger people will disregard Christians who consider animals a peripheral concern:

Many millions of people, especially young people, take kindness towards animals seriously. Jonathan Safran Foer estimates that 18% of US college students describe themselves as vegetarian. Why would such people listen to a church with a reputation for complicity in cruelty? Indeed, one sixth-form evangelist in the UK told me that Christian complicity in animal cruelty is among the most common reasons he hears for rejecting the gospel. Evangelical churches have recently sought to be inclusive, yet few have a policy on animal ethics beyond offering a vegetarian option at church events; some do not even do this. Churches keen to attract the younger generation should take note that this is a serious obstacle to evangelism. Where evangelicals once led their generation in kindness, today's are silent; indeed, some leaders suggest that animal cruelty is not an evangelical concern at all. But God is at work in the world. His groaning creation looks towards restoration when the children of God will be revealed. God can renew His church and soften human hearts. Kindness (Gal. 5:22) is a fruit of the Spirit.[62]

Some Christians who regard pet services as taboo believe that there is a conspiracy of environmentalists, animal advocates and alternate spirituality groups.[63] They are seen as one vanguard for the conspiracy to infiltrate the churches with both religious heresies and secular beliefs in animal rights.

It is difficult to agree with the claims of a conspiracy. Secular animal advocates are disunited in their views having divided into squabbling factions that represent different philosophies: abolitionist, liberationist, welfare, animal rights.[64] Animal rights activists and conservationists have fundamental disagreements with each other. Animal rights activists stress the importance of protecting each individual creature (domestic, agricultural, wild). Environmental conservationists actually reject animal rights, support the eradication of feral animals and concentrate on rescuing representatives of species in danger of extinction.[65]

With respect to the term animal rights it is not necessarily a secular one. The Revd Herman Daggett (1791) and Christian lawyer Lord Erskine (1809) indicated long ago that, without any biblical compromises, we may refer to the 'rights of animals' when thinking about our duties before God toward other creatures. It in no way negates our commitment to the dignity and worth of all humans.[66]

Some Jewish, Muslim, Mormon, New Age, Neo-Pagan, Hindu and Buddhist teachers have discussed their respective beliefs about animals and ethics.[67] Their positive sentiments about animals open up further missional possibilities.

CASE STUDIES

Christians have opportunities to develop creative ministries about animal issues that interact with the wider community. Some well-meaning Christians try to plug gaps caused by a general silence from the pulpits about animals. For example, there is a cottage industry of websites and books collating biblical proof texts on animals and heaven.

The loss of a pet is an emotionally devastating experience. The church's widespread silence on bereavement when a pet dies has prompted self-help writers and followers of alternative spiritualities to fill the vacuum.[68] Dismissive attitudes about sentimental feelings for animals have led health researchers and social workers to talk about 'disenfranchised grief' that is caused when a pet dies.[69] The need for pastoral care of bereaved pet owners is gradually receiving recognition.[70] Australian Uniting Church pastor the Revd Barbara Allen was dubbed the world's first 'animal chaplain' when she was appointed to serve at Melbourne's Lort Smith Animal Hospital which looks after 85,000 animals a year.[71] She offers support to stressed staff and bereaved owners and has officiated at pet blessing services.

A great innovation in American chaplaincy is the inclusion of dogs in ministry to prisoners, house-bound elderly and disabled persons, patients in hospices and mental health facilities, and among children traumatised by domestic violence or who suffer from developmental problems. Michael Koppel remarks:

People involved in care and healing ministries with animals (most particularly, dogs) relate benefits with almost evangelical fervor. Stories abound of care givers and care receivers experiencing profound moments of connection and care.[71]

Jerilyn Felton insists 'it is time for a spiritual/pastoral care provider's working companion to have a wet nose and four feet'.[72]

Another fascinating case concerns the New Skete monastery that was established in 1966 in Cambridge, New York. It is part of the Orthodox Church in America and the monks raise and train German shepherd dogs and offer seminars for owners in the proper care for a dog. New Skete holds a pet blessing service in honour of St Francis of Assisi (October 4).[73]

England's RSCPA will celebrate its bicentenary on Sunday June 16, 2024. This provides a marvellous opportunity for churches to retell the story of Arthur Broome and William Wilberforce as founders of the RSPCA and the biblical witness about animals. Philip has discussed this in more detail in his forthcoming book *The Noah Challenge.*

During the 1970s the Revd Andrew Linzey joined the board of England's RSPCA. In 1975 he drafted a model animal welfare service that anticipated the onset of pet blessing services. Linzey has developed a liturgical book called *Animal Rites* that includes prayers for sick and dying creatures and for many other occasions.[74]

Pet blessing services do open up good connections with local communities. The evangelical Church of Christ in Sydney's northern suburb of North Turramurra agreed a few years ago to have a pet blessing service. The community has been so enthusiastic that the local newspaper reports 'Hundreds flock to church for Sydney pet blessing'.[75] Pastor Richard Oakes declares it is now a 'fixture' for the congregation.

Another well organised community event is hosted by a local Catholic Church:

Our Lady of Fatima Catholic Church Caringbah will hold a St Francis of Assisi pets Mass and mini fair on October 11 at 11 am. Mass to be held on the parish oval. Bring your pet in remembrance of St Francis of Assisi's love for all creatures. After the mass there will be a mini fair with free petting farm, pony rides, rock climbing wall and face painting. All welcome.[76]

St John the Baptist Christian Orthodox Church in Rochester, New York, is part of the Eastern Orthodox family of churches. Once a year, the priest and deacons conduct a liturgical service that celebrates the gift of life to all creatures. It draws together parishioners and pet owners from the local area. A couple of years ago, the local division of the Mounted Police attended and each horse was blessed. The liturgy consists of Trinitarian prayers of praise and thanksgiving for God's creatures, the Lord's Prayer, readings from the Bible, a procession through the church grounds and a ceremonial sprinkling of blessed water on each pet.[77]

It is wise to structure a pet blessing service so that it is theocentric in both worship and thanksgiving. The service should through prayer, scripture, songs, sermon and blessings include these themes:

- Emphasises that God is creator
- Celebrates God's animals in creation
- Gives thanks for the companionship that we enjoy with God's creatures
- Calls for repentance of human cruelty and abuse of animals
- Encompasses animals in the blessed effects of Christ's resurrection
- Foreshadows the peaceable kingdom on a new earth that is to come .

Here is a model sermon outline for a pet blessing service:

Text: Proverbs 12:10: 'Whoever is righteous has regard for the life of his beast but the mercy of the wicked is cruel.'

CHRISTIAN BLESSINGS FOR PETS

The Bible teaches that we have duties and responsibilities toward God's creatures. All creatures ultimately belong to God (Ps.50:10-11; 104:24) and what we do to them reflects on the extent to which we respect or dishonour God. Character studies contrast those who show mercy and care:

- Rebekah shows hospitality to Abraham's servant and cares for his camels (Gen. 24:14, 18-20)
- Jacob worries about the flocks and herds on a long journey (Gen 33:13-14)
- While others who are cruel are marked out:
    Jacob disinherits two sons (Gen 49:5-6) because they were murderers and cruel to oxen
    Balaam is rebuked by the angel for beating his donkey (Num. 22:22-35)
    Samson's cruelty to foxes is a lesson about him as an anti-Adam who rules by violence (Judges 15:4-5)

Several followers of Jesus were the co-founders of England's RSPCA. The Revd Arthur Broome, who ministered among the poor of East London, invited luminaries such as the Christian anti-slave campaigners William Wilberforce and Thomas Fowell Buxton to set up the RSPCA in 1824. They acted on Proverbs 12:10. They cared for both animals and people. Their legacy lives on.

Jesus taught that not one sparrow dies without God watching over it (Matt. 10:29), and he assured us that even as God treasures each sparrow we are also highly cherished (Matt. 10:30-31). We are to bear witness to the Risen Christ who will set free the whole creation (Rom. 8:19-22) and usher in God's peaceful community. The prophets foresaw the day when there will be no violence even among the animals (Isa. 11:6-9).

The heart of the problem of cruelty is the problem of the human heart from which selfish and abusive deeds arise. Jesus offers us the invitation to renewal and a fresh start by becoming his followers. Let us be active agents for Christ in opposing cruelty to all animals.

Let us thank God for the blessing pets bring us through the various stages of life.

THINGS TO DO

You may like to help inspire your local church to oppose the abuse of animals. Look at these passages of scripture: Matt. 10:29; Prov. 12:10; Num. 22:22-34; Gen. 24:14, 18-20; 49:5-6; Judges 15:4-5; Rev. 11: 17-19; Col. 1:15-20. Make a list of key points from these passages and discuss these passages with the worship leaders of your church. Invite the musical team to (a) examine past hymns and songs about animals and (b) challenge the team to compose a new hymn/song that combines animals praising God with the bible's message against cruelty. Set a time-frame for the completion of the lyrics and then the team can teach the congregation this new song.

START THE CONVERSATION

1. 'And I heard every creature in heaven and on earth and under the earth and in the sea, and all that is in them, saying, 'To him who sits on the throne and to the Lamb be blessing and honour and glory and might forever and ever!" (Rev. 5:13). Consider the implications of these words for both our Sunday worship services and our daily habits of life.
2. Discuss with your friends or in a group what does it mean when we say God is caring for and restoring all creation? What pictures does this bring to mind?

10
MARTIAL ARTS, T'AI CHI –
Feet, fist and faith collide?

Sherlock Holmes lives on through all generations. He is the number one fictional character in movie-making history and more than one hundred actors have played him. In the original stories written by Sir Arthur Conan Doyle, Holmes' greatest enemy was the master criminal Professor Moriarty. Their great conflict ended in a fight on the precipice of the Reichenbach Falls in Switzerland. Everyone believed that Holmes had perished but after a few years Doyle 'resurrected' him in the story *The Empty House*. Holmes recounted to Watson how he had survived the fight:

> We tottered together upon the brink of the fall. I have some knowledge, however, of baritsu, or the Japanese system of wrestling, which has more than once been very useful to me. I slipped through his grip, and he with a horrible scream kicked madly for a few seconds and clawed the air with both hands. But for all his efforts he could not get his balance and over he went.[1]

The martial art that Holmes was trained in, however, was not baritsu but 'bartitsu' and Doyle probably picked up a reference to the misspelled word from a newspaper article. Bartitsu did not originate from Japan but was a hybrid art of self-defence that was invented by Edward-William Barton Wright (1860-1951). He blended techniques from English and French boxing as well as others from the Japanese art of jujitsu.[2]

TABOO OR TO DO?

It was during the second half of the twentieth century that a pop cultural fascination developed over martial arts such as judo, karate, tae kwon do, Kung fu, and aikido. Some US soldiers in World War Two were trained in judo and US veterans who fought against the Japanese, and those who served in the Korean War, returned to America having been exposed first-hand to the martial arts as sports.

National and international competitions began in the 1950s. Many were astounded by the feats performed by the Japanese karate champion Masutatsu Oyama such as smashing a stack of thirty roof tiles and breaking two bricks in a single blow. Oyama performed in more than two hundred exhibitions across America which included his being undefeated in all his bouts. He also won unarmed contests against American boxers and wrestlers. Oyama went on to gain a somewhat dubious international reputation for engaging in unarmed battle with a total of fifty-two bulls where he killed three bulls with sudden death blows and snapped off the horns of forty-eight others.

Western pop culture was more widely exposed to the classic martial arts in the 1960s through TV-series that featured characters who fought enemies either in weaponless (unarmed) combat or in the stealthy arts of the ninja fighter using traditional weapons (star darts, wooden staffs and swords). In Australia, fan clubs have been grabbing DVDs for two Japanese syndicated shows with English subtitles that paved the way, *The Samurai* and *Phantom Agents*.

In the mid-1960s, Britain's ITV introduced into the adventure series *The Avengers* the character of Mrs Emma Peel (played by Diana Rigg) who was a scientist and martial arts undercover operative. In 1966 the US network ABC produced a single season of the action hero *The Green Hornet* which included Bruce Lee (1940-1973) in the supporting cast.[3] The great explosion of interest came through the motion pictures from Hong Kong starring Bruce Lee: *The Big Boss, Fists of Fury, The Way of the Dragon, Enter the Dragon*. Around the same time David Carradine starred in the 1970s TV series *Kung Fu*. The 1980s witnessed a franchise of teen-oriented movies known as *The Karate Kid*. *The Matrix* trilogy featured elements of martial arts philosophy as well as major fights. Jackie Chan, Jet Li, Chuck Norris, Steven Seagal and Jean-Claude Van Damme have ridden the crest of the wave in their various films and TV series.

Many Christians are personally involved in the martial arts of judo, karate, Kung fu, tae kwon do and T'ai Chi. Again, on a drive along the highway, one often sees church signs advertising classes in one of the martial arts. The fundamentalist Bob Jones University hosts Champions for Christ which is the university's karate team that performs feats as part of organised evangelistic activities. There are over seven hundred evangelical churches that host as part of their activities Mixed Martial Arts (MMA or cage fighting). The MMA blends kick-boxing, classic wrestling and Brazilian and Thai martial arts. The phenomenon has recently been featured in a film *Fight Church*. Christian retirement living facilities often conduct classes in T'ai Chi to assist the elderly better cope with arthritis and other physical infirmities.

This is an issue where Christians have been polarised by demographics, gender and ages. It is interesting to see how different groups within churches are drawn to or repulsed by particular forms of the martial arts. In blue collar urban areas it is not uncommon to find young Christian men attracted to the 'hard' martial arts (e.g. karate, Kung fu, tae kwon do) while in more white collar suburbs many are attracted to T'ai Chi. Some quarrels have arisen where those who find the 'soft' exercises of T'ai Chi appealing are very alarmed by the tough young 'masculine' Christians who revel in the harder disciplines. There are also some Christians who oppose any kind of martial art for fear of violent behaviour and heretical belief.

BACKGROUND

There are many styles of martial arts. The best known originated from China, Japan and Korea and we are restricting our discussion to examples from these nations as they are perceived and practised in the West. However, there are other kinds of martial arts found in Brazil, Thailand, the Philippines, southern India, parts of Africa, and among New Zealand's Maoris. While we will not be discussing any of those martial arts what we set out in this chapter offers a template for Christians to use when sorting out the critical questions of taboo or to do. The conversation will need to cover, no matter what martial art style we encounter, questions about its spiritual heritage, philosophical precepts, and missional connections.

ZEN MEDITATION AND KARATE

Always more vital to karate than techniques or strength is the spiritual element that lets you move and act with complete freedom. In striving to enter the proper frame of mind Zen meditation is of great importance. Though we say that this meditation involves a state of impassivity and complete lack of thought, we mean that through meditation we can overcome emotion and thinking and give freer reign to our innate abilities than ever before. The Zen state of selflessness is the same condition of disregard for selfish thoughts and concern for personal welfare that the artist experiences in the heart of creation. The man who wants to walk the way of karate cannot afford to neglect Zen and spiritual training.

Masutatsu Oyama, *Vital Karate* (Tokyo; San Francisco: Japan Publications Trading Co, 1967), 8.

There are several spiritual and philosophical influences that we will consider. It is handy to recall that the original spearhead for popular western interest in meditation came via Zen Buddhism. We do not want to rush headlong into talking about Zen but it is one part of the spiritual framework out of which some of the martial arts sprang. There are other spiritual and philosophical influences on the martial arts such as Taoist, Confucian and Shinto beliefs. Taoist thought sprang from the teacher Lao Tzu which emphasises universal harmony through Chi. We discussed the concept of Chi in the chapter on energy healing. Classic martial arts practice mirrors the idea of finding harmony by drawing on the energy of Chi.

Confucian teachings provide part of the philosophical foundation for the precepts of the various martial arts in China and to some extent in Korea and Japan. Confucian thought emphasises the nature of our relationships as they seem to fit into a larger cosmic pattern shaped by the dualities of Yin/Yang, light/dark, sun/moon, male/female, and peace/violence. The true martial artist is one who attains a state of inner harmony with these dualities and does not seek conflict and violence.

The Shinto ('way of the gods') tradition is Japan's native religion which concentrates on honouring specific deities, earthly rulers who represent the deities, and the widespread presence of spirits (kami) which includes one's ancestors. What most westerners do not realise is that sumo wrestling is an ancient martial art that is deeply rooted in Shinto. Sumo contests typically last only a couple of minutes. Wrestlers push, pull, trip and grab each other until one contestant is forced over the ring's perimeter. There are preparatory Shinto rituals which last much longer than the actual bout. One ritual involves the wrestlers stamping their feet in the ring to drive away evil spirits. A salt scattering ritual which is meant to purify the ring is rated just as important as the physical contest. A Shinto priest attends to ensure that every ritual is performed properly.[4]

The shaping of the martial arts owes a lot to these religious traditions, while in China the warrior code of the Shaolin monks reflects Taoist (or Daoist), Confucian and Buddhist influences. In Japan the warrior code of the Samurai was shaped by Shinto beliefs. In both cultures the skills for combat were shaped by these religious and philosophical codes to place restrictions on violence.

The reality is that there is a twofold strand to classical martial arts. One is Chi/ki (energy) which is the key source for the exercise or combat. The other, in particular, is done through Zen or Taoist meditation.

TABOO OR TO DO?

Zen in both its Chinese and Japanese versions comprises a major piece of the puzzle in the development of the classic martial arts. There were pockets of American youth in the 1950s and early 1960s who were attracted to Zen. Followers have since that time popularised the path, experience, and goal of Zen by speaking of the 'moment' or of 'instant calm' when self-realisation is achieved. Zen has its roots in the emergence of Chinese Buddhism, where it is known as Ch'an. Ch'an Buddhism was the principal path of the Shaolin monks who developed Kung fu. Zen holds to the classic Buddhist understanding that there is no God, no mind, and no self: these are illusory. Life is suffering and the great illusion is to be caught up in such suffering. Enlightenment involves breaking the shackles of the rational mind and the chain of thought and experience that binds us to suffering. Zen meditation is the way to achieve the state of enlightenment. The meditative technique includes a place to sit, bodily posture (lotus position, or kneeling), counting breaths and observing one's thoughts. One also may meditate on riddles (or koans) which are so paradoxical they defy rational understanding. A Zen master will use koans to test a student's awareness and ensure that they are not relying on the rational mind to analyse life.

Christmas Humphreys contextualised Zen for the West. He captured the spirit of it in these words:

> Relax. Don't strain, for nothing is worth the while. There is nothing to be found, so why this effort to find it? Sit loose to life, for it flows about you, and if you are wise, you are happily flowing too. Just drop it, whatever it is that is worrying you, and go on dropping it. Laugh and laugh still more; if you cannot, find out why. Walk on![5]

Today's popular meditative practices are fairly light in their demands and are akin to the burden of wearing a baseball cap, whereas one feels the rigour that is required to practise Zen, the feeling of wearing a heavy overcoat.

EXTERNAL AND INTERNAL MARTIAL ARTS

Since the seventeenth century, some practitioners have drawn a distinction between the 'external' and 'internal' martial arts. The division occurred in China during a time of political upheaval with the ruling dynasty favouring one faith more than another. The external arts are designated as those that are physiological in form such as Kung fu and its strong connection to the Shaolin Buddhist monks. The internal arts (called neijing) are principally focused on spiritual exercises associated with the use of Chi/ki, such as T'ai Chi which has a strong affinity with Taoist faith. The dividing line between Taoist and Buddhist faiths has not always been obvious in China's history. However, expert practitioners today still accept the categories of external and internal martial arts.

In Japan the classic words for the martial arts are *budō* and *bujutso*. The term *budō* compounds two words *bu* (war) and *dō* (path or way) and is translated as 'martial way' or 'way of war'. *Bujutso* is likewise a compound word which means the science or art of war. The Japanese word *dō* stems from the Sanskrit term *marga* (path to enlightenment) and refers to a way of life. In Japan the term *budō* has been associated with a spiritual practice that draws together physical, psychological and social elements. In *budō* the way of life is to pursue peace and enlightenment on the understanding that if there is to be peace one must be ready for conflict both externally and internally.

Jujitsu and Judo

Jujitsu (meaning flexible) is one of Japan's oldest martial arts and has a variety of styles or schools. It incorporates grabbing an opponent and throwing techniques. Tournaments in East Asia may also make use of weapons such as swords, the sai (a fork-dagger), and nunchaku (made famous by Bruce Lee). However in many countries the nunchaku is a prohibited weapon. Jujitsu has no single founder but an early version known as Ryoi-Shinto ryu emerged in the seventeenth century that was associated with the wandering Samurai teacher Hichirouemon Masakatsu Fukono. In Ryoi-Shinto the jujitsu fighter would strike blows aimed at the body's pressure points or energy centres that lie at the heart of the theory of acupuncture.

Jujitsu gave birth to the art of judo as a sport in the late nineteenth century. Judo is another martial art where one grabs an opponent knocks them off-balance using open hands, arms and legs. Unlike jujitsu there are no tournaments using weapons.

Karate

Karate is what Western pop culture knew first. Elvis Presley was studying karate long before the West ever heard of Bruce Lee and kung fu. Karate, which means empty hand, involves a lot more than spectacular feats of smashing roof tiles and bricks. It originated in the island of Okinawa as a discipline of combat without using weapons and individual contests involved very bruising physical contact. One studies karate under a teacher (sensei) whom the pupil honours and obeys. Gichin Funakoshi introduced karate to mainland Japan in 1922 and in the years leading up to World War Two most Japanese citizens had daily sessions in practising karate and other martial arts. In that context the training was strongly rooted not just in Shinto and Zen influences but it also served the political aims of the military government.

Since World War Two three categories of karate have developed:

- Traditional karate places an emphasis on the physical skills of combat, the traditional relationship of teacher-pupil and the spiritual discipline of meditation.
- Sports karate involves contestants scoring points but without physically striking an opponent.
- Full-contact karate involves physical contact in sports contests but contestants wear protective gear such as padded boots, shin-guards and gloves.

Kung Fu

Kung fu refers to concentration. Most westerners first heard about kung fu by watching David Carradine on TV or Bruce Lee's films. The martial art precursors to kung fu are traced back to the twelfth century BC. Pupils belonged to a school and were taught the art by a teacher (sifu). In its classic historical setting a pupil studied the underlying religious philosophy (Taoist, Confucian, and Buddhist) and meditative techniques alongside the physical exercises. The emphasis was on following a strict regimen of personal sacrifice and self-discipline.

Many of the physical techniques of kung fu derived from observing insects and animals fighting. This is echoed in various classic fighting styles such as the monkey, white crane, and praying mantis. It has carried over into the nickname of 'grasshopper' for David Carradine's character Kwai Chang Caine. Bruce Lee was known as the little dragon.

DAVID CARRADINE'S CREDO

The real essence of kung fu is not self-defense but philosophy ... Kung fu is a total way of life, of which personal combat is the least significant segment. The spiritual teaching will go far beyond the physical aspects of kung fu, enhance all those advantages and provide much more: harmony with and understanding of the true nature of the Cosmos we live in; triumph over most human problems—disease, misfortune and even death. There is no end to the student's potential gain. What you put in is what you get out. Happiness depends on mental health and inner peace more than any outside factors. Kung fu study promotes inner peace, mental health, strength, fortitude, patience.

David Carradine, *Spirit of Shaolin*
(Sydney: Random House, 1991), 5 & 6.

Bruce Lee had a spiritual-philosophical angle to his style of kung fu known as Jeet Kune Do (jeet means intercepting; kune means fist; do means style). Lee's textbook *Chinese Kung Fu: The Philosophical Art of Self Defence* presented traditional Chinese spiritual belief. He taught this philosophy in California to his students including actors such as James Coburn and James Garner.

His spiritual philosophy was showcased in words and deeds in *Enter The Dragon*. In 2001 an uncut DVD version was released and introduced by his widow Linda Lee. She explained that Bruce's ideas were contained in some dialogue that had been cut out of the 1973 cinema release. In the uncut version Bruce Lee discusses the martial arts with the 'teacher' at the Shaolin monastery. The teacher remarked, 'Your skills are at the point of spiritual insight.' When the teacher asked what he thinks about an opponent, Lee affirmed in true Ch'an/Zen style that 'there is no opponent because the word "I" does not exist.'[6] In a separate scene Lee taught a teenage boy a rudimentary point illustrating it with a classic Buddhist reference: the finger that points to the moon. The student's focus in training must not be on the finger or he will miss the glories of heaven.

Kung fu fighting encompasses the use of one's body (head, shoulders, elbows, fists, knees and feet) in striking blows, blocking and defending. It has historically included the use of various weapons (e.g. axes, bow and arrow, knives, spears, wooden staffs, swords). Kung fu came to prominence during the Ming dynasty when the Buddhist monk Chueh Yuan is credited with introducing it to the Shaolin monastery. The Shaolin martial arts featured training in both using the wooden staff as a weapon and hand (unarmed) combat. In Shaolin temples icons of the deity Vajrapāni featured him holding the staff as a symbolic representation of divine protection. All forms of combat were shaped by an emphasis on Buddhist clerical activities, symbols, and meditative methods that included chanting sutras (verses from sacred texts). The Shaolin monks also linked kung fu to Taoist bodily practices for attaining health and spiritual enlightenment.

The monastic community studied kung fu partly as a spiritual discipline and partly as a means of defending their temple from bandits. Shaolin monk soldiers served in battles on behalf of the Tang and Ming dynasties. This close association with the Emperors ended when the Manchu dynasty came to power.[7]

In modern times various schools of kung fu have emerged that offer a diversity of spiritual emphases and different styles of combat. An eclectic approach to kung fu thought and practice has emerged among different teachers with a distinctly western cultural outlook.

Tae Kwon Do

Tae kwon do developed in Korea and the three words mean: Tae to kick or strike with the foot; Kwon refers to punching; Do means art. Tae kwon do has its roots in earlier martial art traditions that were present in early Korean history. Korea was once divided into three smaller kingdoms and in the sixth century AD the King of Silla, Chin-Huang, strengthened his military force by having them taught a martial art. That story is regarded by strict practitioners as the root source for what eventually developed into tae kwon do. Korean versions of Confucian, Taoist and Buddhist thought provided an important framework for the development of Korea's martial arts. Since the 1970s tae kwon do has gained in worldwide popularity as a tournament sport.

T'ai Chi Chuan

Most people today think of T'ai Chi as a gentle form of exercise associated with elderly practitioners. The term T'ai Chi Chuan means supreme ultimate fist. The reference to 'supreme ultimate' harkens back to the Taoist concept of Yin and Yang which we discussed in the energy healing chapter. The term 'fist' is an integral part of the classic discipline because it was originally a martial art that even included the use of double-edged swords.

T'ai Chi uses a variety of bodily postures many of which are named after animal poses such as the crane. Unlike the rapid movements in karate and tae kwon do, T'ai Chi involves deliberate slow exercises which represent a continuous flowing action of harmony and energy.

CONTACT POINTS

We have noted that the martial arts are found in films, TV programmes, gymnasiums, sports tournaments, as well as community and church halls. It is only rivalled by yoga in terms of appeal and adherents. A few isolated Christian apologists who write about cults have from time-to-time produced booklets or brief chapters condemning all martial arts because of their roots in Chinese and Japanese religions.[8] However, it is strange that there has been very little in-depth or widespread Christian discussion and preaching about the martial arts.

DISCERNMENT

The primary discernment issue is that the martial arts have a historical and philosophical link to the concept of Chi/ki as universal energy. The East Asian martial arts have also been shaped by Shinto, Taoist, Confucian and Buddhist teachings and meditative practices. We have previously discussed Chi and universal energy in the chapters about energy healing, aromatherapy and yoga. It seems appropriate to remind ourselves that the questions of those chapters remain relevant when looking at the martial arts.

The key point remains: is it appropriate to be involved in a Chi-based practice that affirms an impersonal universal energy? A committed practitioner will harness the power of Chi as well as rebounding that back on the attacker/opponent. Martial artists who believe in Chi as a spiritual reality understand that what takes place between two people is a microscopic reflection of a larger cosmic reality. The two contestants reflect the polar principles referred to in Chinese beliefs about Yin/Yang, light/dark, male/female etc. This is in contrast to the Christian worldview which does not accept that there are dual eternal processes or powers or beings. Christianity does not uphold the belief that we are all part of impersonal universal energy. God is a personal creator and, while good and evil co-exist, they are not ultimate or eternal forces.

In the training halls (called dojos) where instructors teach karate there are ceremonial rituals at the start and finish of a session. The pupils sit on their knees, they usually bow to the teacher and are asked to spend time in meditation. To an outsider the ritual ceremonies of bowing may appear to involve a religious activity. In western cultures a bow to a monarch or saluting another dignitary has always been regarded as a mark of respect but not as an act of worship. Contrary to grass-roots claims among some Christians, the ritual bowing in karate and kung fu is not an act of worship but reflects the peculiar cultural protocols in Japan and China of respecting another person. In some dojos a ceremonial bow may also be directed to the photograph of a teacher who has died. The teacher and pupils say 'thank you' using the Japanese words when speaking to each other. The ritual also signifies the roles of the participants who in the training session learn to respect their teacher and sparring partner. The training session involves the control of bodily movements that signifies personal restraint from aggression.[9]

The ceremonial meditative exercise may go in various directions depending upon the teacher and the degree to which a religious philosophy is taught. In some dojos the meditative exercise may be devoid of any religious trimmings and acts as a way of merely focusing thoughts. In other cases one might be in a dojo where Zen is central. The 'no God,' 'no-mind' and 'no self' position of Zen is radically different from the Christian understanding: God, the human mind and self are not illusory.

The conservative *Christian Research Journal* is an apologetics publication noted for analysing matters through the grid of heresy. The journal addressed the question of Christians in the martial arts and picked up the same issue of discernment that we addressed in the yoga chapter: just because a discipline has certain origins does this immediately rule it out? The authors advise this is committing the error of the genetic fallacy: 'this error assumes that since the origin of a belief or practice was wrong, despite its development, it is still wrong today.'[10] Years ago Pat Means counselled university students to apply the following criteria to a practitioner or discipline:

- What is the philosophy behind the discipline? What is the underlying view of reality?
- How does that philosophy compare with the Christian view of life?
- Is the philosophy communicated essential to the practice? Is it communicated directly or indirectly?
- How would you describe the feelings that you derive from the experience? Are you left with a sense of oneness?
- What are the outcomes of this discipline for Christian spiritual growth and discipleship?[11]

From our perspective, with respect to martial arts, the question will be, is the practitioner or the group at large clearly saying that the eastern background outlined above is integral to the training?

Some western practitioners of martial arts believe that training is 'a form of spiritual practice' to enable their personal development and it may bring them 'closer to enlightenment'.[12] These practitioners regard the martial arts as a pathway to enlightenment and blend the training with eclectic beliefs about self-improvement and spirituality. One social researcher reports that some European martial artists insist that they are more interested in the spirituality of karate and aikido than the Japanese.[13]

What is new in this discernment section is the issue of violence. In the training and practice of the external martial arts the concern is that there is aggression and violence. Should the Church be associated with it?

Ross was recently in Fiji, a largely Christian country and was informed by their Prime Minister, and other prominent officials, that their major homeland concern is domestic violence. He shared that it is a major concern for other western nations. In

Australia family violence is a national epidemic with one in three women affected in their lifetime and around eighty women killed every year.[14] Churches are asking to what extent does ministry in any way, even indirectly, perpetuate violence.

Churches that sponsor martial arts groups should sift through some critical questions about violence, aggression and masculinity. Lessons may be learned by glancing at history. For example, masculine prowess and athleticism was celebrated in ancient Rome's entertainment industry. The Coliseum was the stadium where the crowds were amused by brutal blood sports that culminated in killing humans and animals and the early Christians were martyred. The message of Jesus eventually triumphed over violent persecution and the gladiatorial blood-sports.

For centuries British culture emphasised being 'manly' and 'muscular'. The virtue of 'proving' manhood criss-crossed all social classes and was often cruelly manifested in harsh business activity, tough child-rearing and rugged forms of recreation. Manhood and masculinity was wrapped up in activities that celebrated spilling blood in field sport and in hunting animals. In the nineteenth century a year-long debate occurred between E. A. Freeman and Anthony Trollope about manliness being proved in aggressive sport and in fox-hunting.[15] The brutal treatment of slaves and cruelty shown toward children and animals goaded Christian reformers such as William Wilberforce and Lord Shaftesbury to challenge myths of manhood that celebrated aggression and cruelty.

A movement called 'Muscular Christianity' that was spearheaded by the Revd Charles Kingsley (1819-1875) sought to represent a more rugged image of Jesus than that revealed in the sentimental lyrics of some hymns and 'gentle Jesus meek and mild' of Christian art. It crystallised when faith and athletic prowess were linked to prominent sportsmen such as the cricketer C.T. Studd (1862-1931) and Rugby Union player and Olympic Games athlete Eric Liddell (1902-1945). Liddell's story was dramatised in the bio-movie *Chariots of Fire*. Both men left the limelight of sport to become missionaries.

Some Christians believe that linking feet, fist and faith is in the spirit of what Studd and Liddell stood for. However, the advent of MMA in churches has raised critical concerns that it is a brutal activity where the winner 'proves' his or her superiority by battering his or her opponent into submission. It is much more than a cricket or rugby match! Some MMA fans claim that the risk of being fatally injured is low. Practitioners cannot overlook the fact that during a contest in Ireland in 2016 the Portuguese MMA fighter Joao Carvalho died of brain injury.[16] Critics point out the great difficulty in reconciling this aggressive activity with the teaching of Jesus and manifesting the fruit of the Spirit.[17]

Apart from exploring a more muscular Christianity another reason people take up martial art training is for personal safety.[18] It is not surprising that many women study a martial art because of fears of being assaulted. Unrestrained violence in western society is manifested in gang sub-cultures and criminal enterprises, acts of terror, alcohol-fuelled fights at pubs, school-yard bullying, and in domestic contexts where women, children, the elderly and companion pets are assaulted.

In such training one is taught the martial arts as a form of self-defence, yet exercising self-restraint. The ascetic training in the traditional martial arts inculcated a moral code to restrain and curb violence which was shaped by the precepts of the Taoist, Confucian, Buddhist and Shinto ways of life. The essence of restraint in the 'warrior's code' is popularly expressed in the best-selling fantasy trilogy *The Chronicles of Thomas Covenant, The Unbeliever*:

> Do not hurt where holding is enough;
> Do not wound where hurting is enough;
> Do not maim where wounding is enough;
> And kill not where maiming is enough;
> The greatest warrior is one who does not need to kill.[19]

However, in contrast to the code, the martial arts action hero movies morally justify violence and a lack of real self-restraint on the basis they are achieving a greater community good. In *Enter The Dragon* Bruce Lee confronts the crime and corruption perpetrated by Mr Han's martial arts academy. Han is a renegade of the Shaolin community who has perverted the way of Kung fu. The Shaolin teacher places the burden of restoring the temple's honour on Lee's shoulders. Lee also learns that his sister committed suicide when she was surrounded by Han's henchmen. Lee defeats dozens of henchmen through superior fighting techniques but also kills both Han and Han's chief bodyguard. He kills the bodyguard to avenge his sister's death. Lee's casualties perish in a spree of violence and his vengeance causes him to step outside the Shaolin code.

Many American martial arts films, particularly those starring Steven Seagal and Jean-Claude Van Damme, emphasise a theme that crossed over from Wild West and police crime-busting movies. The individual stands outside the law and avenges wrongs by using violence in order to vanquish evil. The message is that the individual brings good and wins through aggression. This was epitomised in the classic western movie *The Man Who Shot Liberty Valance* where John Wayne told Jimmy Stewart that out in the untamed Wild West a man solves his own problems by using a gun and brute force. The same point is emphasised in modern police stories such as the Dirty Harry movies starring Clint Eastwood and the *Die Hard* movies starring Bruce Willis.

The Karate Kid is less violent but remains a typical Hollywood morality tale that contains lessons about (a) personal happiness is a reward for self-effort and (b) bad guys will not be rewarded. The story is about a teenage boy being bullied by aggressive peers who use karate to intimidate. It contrasts the use of karate for self-improvement with the bullies' misuse of it. The boy undergoes personal growth when an elderly Japanese man teaches him discipline, restraint, self-esteem and moral principles through karate. The bullies are vanquished in a refereed karate sports contest.

This pop cultural message about revenge and overcoming violence with violence stands in tension with biblical teaching for the followers of Jesus that:

- The resurrection of Christ signifies God's 'no' to the violence that led to Jesus' crucifixion. The resurrection is not just an event but opens up a new way of grace-filled living in the present that repudiates treating others as non-persons. Christians are meant to be persons of peace who manifest the fruit of the spirit (Gal. 5:16-26), bless others by being peacemakers (Matt. 5:9) and love their neighbour, even after wronged (Mark 12:28-34).The essence of Jesus' teaching as vindicated by the resurrection is a non-violent way of living.[20]
- The ultimate right to mete out vengeance on evil-doers belongs to God (Deut. 32:35; Ps. 94:1; Rom. 12:19; Heb. 10:30). Vengeance is personally destructive and not for the disciple of Jesus. As one doctor told us 'it's not what you eat that kills you but what is eating you!'
- Jesus' sober words that those who live by the spirit of the sword die by the sword (Matt. 26:52).

There are many reasons why followers of Jesus adopt the martial arts. Some affirm the benefits of learning self-defence and fitness. Others speak of the positive social bonds formed by belonging to a martial arts group. With passive martial arts like T'ai Chi there are physical health and well-being benefits. There are also missional outreach opportunities. Many students who learn self-defence techniques affirm that they are in the process of becoming a better person.

As this chapter outlines the discernment will be twofold: is the training as it is practiced still overtly linked to Eastern spiritual beliefs, and does it promote violence? The other issue for reflection is what is the teacher's worldview with respect to these two points? The answer to these three questions will assist in sorting out is this 'taboo or to do?'

CASE STUDIES

One reason why the topic needs to be addressed is that many followers of Jesus are looking for help in coping with life's pressures. We regularly receive phone calls where the person wants to know if it is 'ok' as a Christian to be exploring a particular martial art. One recent case involved a man who said that he was under enormous stress through work and it was impacting on his marriage. He had not found a church counselling session very helpful and had started classes in a martial art known as Qi-Gong, which he said was like a lifeline for coping. We had a pastoral concern about whether the martial art training was a helpful outlet for releasing pent-up aggression or was he learning skills to physically lash out? It is this kind of pastoral conversation that churches can engage in.

One of the most interesting characters that we have come across in church life today is Fighting Father Dave, who with others started the Order of the Fighting Fathers. He is best known for his work with at risk youth especially in his use of boxing and martial arts. He is an ordained Anglican minister and a professional boxer who holds a six-degree black belt and the world record for the longest boxing stint. His parish is inner city where he has served for many years. Dave Smith's model is not dissimilar to those of others operating an external martial art ministry in a missional framework where there are benefits felt in the community.

At the present time he focuses on boxing. He has turned his church hall into a boxing ring and three nights a week for three hours has training for thirty adults and youth. It is open to everyone. This leads to his weekend camps known as a 'warrior weekend'. Each training session is preceded by a prayer session. It is based on the Benedictine pattern of prayer every three hours starting from 6 am to 6 pm. The prayer is a mixture of silent prayer and community reflection. It is then followed by physical training and exercise as well as boxing techniques. As Father Dave points out this programme can be replicated with martial arts as he has himself done. His programme receives government funding as it is seen as assisting young people to overcome violent extremism and sectarianism, as Christian and Muslim youth from the margins train and interact with each other.

For Father Dave the key concern is violence. He ensures that the East Asian spiritual issues spoken about in this chapter don't take root in his ministry. However he is quick to remind one that the key is the trainer and what they bring to the ring about spirituality and physical violence. He goes out of his way to ensure he is not equipping people to be street fighters but is offering a cathartic outlet. Instead his passion is for building up sporting prowess, confidence and identifying strengths and weaknesses in character. In particular the training incorporates life therapy for 'kids on the edge' who are facing addictions and the like. He believes it is essential that churches involved in this ministry have trainers who can discern those in the programme who have ego problems and unresolved anger issues as they tend to seek those skills for violent purposes.

Father Dave's ministry has so impacted the local community that Marrickville Council have twice awarded him 'citizen of the year' and he has been nominated for 'Australian of the Year'. In his ministry he does not practise external martial arts or boxing with no physical contact as this is like learning swimming strokes without being in a pool. What Father Dave is doing is not unique to his local area but it is a ministry that is found around the world.[21]

We know of several churches that have incorporated T'ai Chi into their life and ministry. It tends to develop under the canopy of a creative living programme operated by volunteer parishioners who teach painting, sketching, jewellery making, dancing and a variety of learning activities such as T'ai Chi.

A helpful model is St Martin's, Walsall. The Vicar, the Revd Simon Bickersteth, described to us the 'St Martin's T'ai Chi' ministry.[22]

'We're on a busy road, so thousands of people pass by the church every single day, and are easy to reach, being on several busy bus routes. We also have excellent facilities, which are used by a wide range of different community groups.

It is clear to everyone who comes into our facilities that we are a Christian place of worship. If we have enquiries about hiring our halls, which we feel conflict with the values of the Christian faith, we will turn down those lettings. For example in the past we were approached by a local 'healing' group to ask if they could use our halls as a place where people can receive healing, using things such as crystals, reiki, etc. We explained to them that we would not allow our facilities to be used for such activities, because they went against the teaching of scripture. Likewise we would not allow people to hold Halloween parties in our facilities.

A karate group that meets at St Martin's, and is a group that hires the hall but does not have any direct link with the church.

The T'ai Chi groups however are run by several members of St Martin's Church. These groups have been going now for quite a number of years, and it is run specifically with the aim of helping improve flexibility and movement in older people.

Around eight years ago, we launched a weekly community café, to provide a place for people in the local community to meet. This was in response to recognition that there were a lot of older people living in the local community around the church, many of whom live on their own, and we wanted to try and build links with the wider community, and address some of the issues of loneliness and isolation that exist in the area.

The T'ai Chi groups were introduced alongside the weekly community café. The groups have proved very popular. The leaders have very gently allowed their faith to impact the people who attend the T'ai Chi group. So for example, we have a prayer board where people can pin their prayer requests – this is always available when the T'ai Chi group meets. People who attend this group know that because of this they are being prayed for, and they know they can ask for prayer at any time.

As a result of the café and the T'ai Chi group, relationships have been formed, and through these relationships we have seen people coming to faith, or returning to faith, and some have started worshipping at St Martin's. And for those who don't worship at St Martin's, by belonging to the T'ai Chi groups they still feel part of the wider St Martin's Church family.'

THINGS TO DO

Do a web-search on levels of violence in your local area. Then look at what your church and others are doing about responding to that violence in their teaching pastoral ministry. Identify churches and Christian groups involved in martial arts in your area and work out what are their motivations. Is the hall rented for martial arts or is it part of their own ministry?

START THE CONVERSATION

1. Your group may not feel comfortable with external martial arts. Discuss whether a masculine spirituality is authentic? If so, what shape would that take at Dave Smith's Warrior Weekend?
2. Among your friends share personal stories of violent and abusive behaviour that you have observed or been touched by. Can one justify external martial arts in such a culture?
3. In your group or church context explore the question would you include T'ai Chi in a creative arts lifestyle programme? If so, would there be any boundaries?

CONTINUING THE CONVERSATION ...

Why this book? There was an uncanny moment as we were starting to write these final pages. The radio was on in the background when the host started interviewing an entertainment journalist. The feature story was on an admired actor who has reappeared having been out of the limelight for some years but had re-emerged with two new movies. Although at one time successful she had faded from view as her personal life imploded. This included the collapse of a difficult marriage. Her return to the big screen flowed out of her journey of self-discovery. For her the way forward had come through taking up yoga with a spirit guide. She shared that all the negative energy in her life had been released. The radio host, journalist and talk-back callers all celebrated the exciting news and shared how marvellous yoga is for coping with the passages of life. Her story of finding new hope in the spiritual disciplines is the same story for so many people today.

In this book we have shared this is our world today. In a spiritual, but less Christian, world we and our neighbours encounter global spiritual disciplines many of which originate from sources whose origins are not part of the Christian worldview. The constant question for followers of Jesus is 'taboo or to do?' It is a decision all of us make as we engage in conversation with our friends, family and neighbours. We will need to revisit some of the principles that have been discussed.

While the modern church is grappling with important theological debates such as new perspectives on Paul, the

Christian's grass-roots experience is more likely to be an encounter with 'taboo or to do' topics. It will be at our peril if we simply march to the tune of doctrinal issues but fail to pay attention to the lifestyle journey questions that we are facing in our own lives and community. If we look back at the chapters they deal with issues of connecting, caring and responding to things that we value. They also cover matters of finding guidance for living. These are the big questions for today.

As we have explored in the chapter dealing with forbidden paths or helpful bridges, some have just not lived out the conversation, or the issue of 'taboo or to do,' in their individual lives and church environment. Another step has been taken by incarnationally reaching into environments like new spirituality festivals.

We should take heart that we are not orphans as this kind of conversation is not new to the church. If one lives in Asia or other thriving melting pots the interaction between different spiritualities in every day experience is simply normal. The church in its history has had to make 'taboo or to do' decisions. We illustrated this in 'Starting the Conversation' where we explored the 'Pagan' connections with Christmas and Easter.

Another historical example is found in medieval times when Pope Gregory wrote a letter (601 AD) to the Abbot Mellitus on a 'taboo or to do' matter namely to keep or to destroy existing Pagan temples. Pope Gregory was keen not to give credence to idolatry and anything demonic however, the considered view was

> The best modern evangelism goes where people are and listens, binds together prayer and truth, celebrates the goodness and complexity of life as well as judging the sinfulness of evil, and sees truth as something to be done and experienced as well as to be intellectually believed. It walks in humility.'
>
> John Finney, *Recovering the Past: Celtic and Roman Mission* (London: Darton, Longman & Todd, 1996), 47.

not to destroy the buildings because of the negative impression this may have on the people. The advice he gave was to ritually purify the temples by removing idols and prayerfully rededicating the buildings to the worship of God. He was building a bridge by Christianising the venues and opening the way for faith. He urged a measured and gradual response that would encourage people to attend services rather than expecting that all errors in Pagan belief would immediately vanish.[1]

The first reason why this book is because it is a 'taboo or to do' world for the followers of Jesus. The questions come into sharp focus in our evangelism and missional encounters.

A second reason is apparent as one explores the topics. We come from different cultures and backgrounds as individuals and Christian communities. Some have no problem with Hallowe'en but have great concerns about T'ai Chi. Others let their church hall for karate but may be totally opposed to yoga. Others embrace yoga but are gravely concerned about Mindfulness meditation. These variances are found in different church affiliations and cultural settings. What is accepted as 'kosher' in America may be rejected in England or Australia. However it is important that we listen to each other and understand why as individuals and Christian communities we have responded differently. Through that listening we may be challenged to abandon one practice and embrace another.

A third reason is pastoral. People of all persuasions are seeking to be the best person they can possibly be. We seek to enrich that journey by raising issues of discernment and assisting the reader to understand the background of spiritual disciplines. Ultimately relying on Scripture, prayer, guidance and the input of our believing community, we can make our own informed response. As we have personally explored the case studies and the background to the topics our own ideas and preconceptions have been challenged. For example, Hallowe'en in America is quite dissimilar to how we understand it but those insights have helped us to consider new horizons. We have previously expressed general concerns about Mindfulness but we have been prompted to reflect on the journey of those who have sought to place it beyond Buddhism and into a Christian and missional context. Those who assisted us in discussing issues have said that they too have had to rethink and reflect. Others have felt 'guilty' about the advice they may have given. We have found it an enriching experience. A good sermon to be alive must first speak to the preacher and we sense the same for a book and all those who share in its production.

A fourth reason is that this is not an encyclopedia of life, the universe and everything. Spiritual practices and influences come and go and just as Mindfulness surprised by its quickly attained global influence so some new fad or discipline may appear. The basic principles we have sought to explore in the book have application to other contested issues that may arise. It is also applicable to other disciplines such as the relationship between psychology and pastoral care.

A final reason is the need for the Christian community to show maturity and take a lead here. It is a syncretistic world and what does it mean to be a true follower of Jesus? How do we exercise Christ-honouring discipleship without 'demonising' other ways of approaching life? When is it appropriate to adopt or reject other traditions? Beyond the Christian community the world around us also witnesses similar processes. In some East Asian cultures there is a tendency to warmly absorb a wide tapestry of traditions. China is the great example of absorbing Confucian, Taoist and Buddhist traditions, while in the turbulence of the Middle East, the pendulum swings toward an ISIL destruction of anything deemed contrary to its authority or contaminating influences on its culture. What we believe is valuable is to steer a different course that is faithful to the way of Jesus.

LIVING IN THE CONVERSATION

To constructively continue the conversation, consider again some of the steps that have come to the fore through the pages of this book and people sharing their narrative and case studies. This is not a recipe for unpacking everything that is said. A conversation rather than a rigid formula is needed.

Step one: Reflect on how Christians have responded to these issues in the past. In the chapter 'Starting the Conversation' we identified six particular styles: heresy, spiritual warfare, cultural, end-time conspiracy, testimony, and incarnational. What styles do I, or my Christian community, bring to table for conversation? There may be more than one and they may differ from one conversation to another. There may be other styles that we add to the grid. If the postmodern world has taught us anything it is that we need to know where we are coming from and what has influenced us. For example, some may be committed to spiritual warfare and have an aversion to the martial arts but not be concerned about aromatherapy. Without losing the dimension of being engaged in a spiritual realm am I open to the further steps?

Step two: Consider whether we should prohibit, Christianise, or wholeheartedly embrace the discipline. In this context there is the need to ponder whether the practice may be separated from its origin? Or has it so evolved from its roots that it is neutral? In the conversation between communities of faith and Christians this will be at the heart of it. If there is no decision made the likelihood is that one will drift into a position. Healthy churches have healthy conversations. It is this practical conversation that people in our churches are crying out for but without being trapped by a legalist approach. John Drane points out, as far as evangelism is concerned, the postmodern person has a need for 'practical information' and, if you are not addressing the issues which specifically deal with your time, you are not preaching the gospel at all.[2]

Step three: Appreciate the role of the practitioner. The actor we mentioned above was not only exploring yoga but doing so with an Eastern spirituality guide. It appears to those we have interacted with that the spirituality of the practitioner is just as important as the practice itself.

Step four: Seek to be consistent. We acknowledge that individuals, churches and denominations are taking different positions in response to disciplines which partly reflect the broad nature of the church. However, it is apparent that most of us are inconsistent; we have a positive position on one discipline that is inconsistent with our standing on another. So we might find ourselves embracing T'ai Chi but placing a ban on yoga, or be open to Hallowe'en events but scoff at the blessing of animals. These mixed stances are confusing for those seeking to grow in Christian discipleship.

Step five: Embrace the resurrection embodiment. Christian living is resurrection living. Christ is the first-fruits of the harvest (1 Cor. 15:17): as it was for him, so it us for us. He was raised and transformed but a whole person. Therefore God sees us as whole persons both now and in eternity. We are whole people so in the conversation we must also consider the extent to which these practices enrich our entire being. People are drawn to mind-body-spirit festivals as they believe the exhibitors and presenters will assist them in developing a holistic way of life. The conversation should centre in a holistic spiritual embodiment.

N. T. Wright raises our vision:

> Rather, it is that with the resurrection of Jesus God's new world has begun; in other words, his being raised from the dead is the start, the paradigm case, the foundation, the beginning, of that great setting-right which God will do for the whole cosmos at the end. The risen body of Jesus is the one bit of the physical universe that has already been 'set right'. Jesus is therefore the one through whom everything else will be 'set right'.[3]

Step six: Explore incarnational mission. Words to this effect are often expressed 'A ship is safest when it is in its port. But that's not what ships were made for.'[4] We were reborn to sail beyond the church harbour. The conversation cannot be contained within the Christian community as it is being lived out in our media, festivals, gyms, workplaces, schools, universities, and sports teams. We have been learning about the importance of incarnational living and practicing proximity and presence with people. This is where the conversation will be shaped and the growth of the kingdom determined. The spirit of the conversation is one of gentleness and respect (1 Peter 3:15). As we discern what God is already up to in people's lives we co-operate with that.

Finally, relying on God's direction, reflect on what it means to live a relevant and meaningful Christian life. There are no 'no-go' zones for God.

Barry was a prominent sports television presenter and radio talk-back host. We first met at a mind-body-spirit festival where he told his story. His life was mess due to a domestic problem and did not like himself at all. He was looking for a way forward. He was an irregular attendee of his local evangelical church. On his radio show he often had an astrologer and spiritual director who rated well with the audience but he privately thought he was a joke. At this point of crisis Barry listened to the astrologer who helped him come to terms with his life and they became friends. What he discovered through astrology and other practices transformed his life. He eventually trained in astrology and went on to become an influential spiritual counsellor using the disciplines set out in this book. Whilst his church failed to meet Barry's need at the time, we and others built a bridge that enabled a positive dialogue to continue with him. By creating the dialogue on the religious practices and traditions explored in this book, we not only inform and empower ourselves, we open the door to broader conversations in our neighbourhoods.

Let the writer of Hebrews have the final word:

> Pray for us, for we are sure that we have a clear conscience, desiring to act honourably in all things ... Now may the God of peace who brought again from the dead our Lord Jesus, the great shepherd of the sheep, by the blood of the eternal covenant, equip you with everything good that you may do his will, working in us that which is pleasing in his sight, through Jesus Christ, to whom be glory forever and ever. Amen. (Heb. 13:18, 20-21).

NOTES

STARTING THE CONVERSATION

1. For example, see the Barna Group, *Perceptions of Jesus, Christians & Evangelism in England* (Executive Report 2015). This report was commissioned by the Church of England and the Evangelical Alliance. The survey found that 40% do not believe that Jesus was a real person, and only 25% believe that Jesus was God in human form.
2. Marcus Jones, 'Weekly Church of England attendance drops below one million,' at www.premier.org.uk/News/UK/Weekly-Church-of-England-attendance-drops-below-one-million.html
3. Theos, 'executive summary' *The Spirit of Things Unseen: belief in post-religious Britain* (London: Theos, 2013), 7.
4. Theos, 7.
5. See the summary of the report http://www.norc.org/PDFs/GSS%20Reports/GSS_Religion_2014.pdf
6. Jeff Brumley, 'As Millennials leave the church, some youth ministers ponder 'scary stats,' https://baptistnews.com/2016/04/18/as-millennials-leave-the-church-some-youth-ministers-ponder-scary-stats/
7. Diana Butler Bass, 'Oprah's new 'Belief' series shows how dramatically the nature of faith is shifting' in *The Washington Post* available at https://www.washingtonpost.com/news/acts-of-faith/wp/2015/10/18/oprahs-new-belief-series-shows-how-dramatically-the-nature-of-faith-is-shifting/
8. Elizabeth Gilbert, *Eat Pray Love* (New York: Penguin, 2006), 206.
9. Mark McCrindle, *Australians and Religion*, McCrindle Research, October 2011. Diagram used with permission.
10. Michelle Boorstein, 'Some are writing obituaries for American religion. Krista Tippett is documenting its revolution,' *Washington Post*, April 6 2016 available at https://www.washingtonpost.com/news/acts-of-faith/wp/2016/04/06/donald-trump-black-lives-matter-cosmology-all-signs-religion-is-alive-and-well-to-krista-tippett/
11. Ed Stetzer, 'Nominal Christians are becoming more secular, and that's creating a startling change for the U.S.' in *The Washington Post* available at https://www.washingtonpost.com/news/acts-of-faith/wp/2015/11/04/nominal-christians-becoming-more-secular-and-thats-creating-a-startling-change-for-the-us/
12. Theos, 23.
13. Philip Johnson, 'The Aquarian Age and Apologetics,' *Lutheran Theological Journal* 34 (2000): 51-60; and, 'Apologetics, Mission and New Religious

Movements: A Holistic Approach,' *Lutheran Theological Journal* 36 (2002): 99-111.
14. The model remains very current in thinking about doctrine and mission see Justin S. Holcomb, 'The Truth About Heresy,' *Christianity Today* October 2015: 38-46.
15. Irving Hexham, Stephen Rost and John W. Morehead eds. *Encountering New Religious Movements: A Holistic Evangelical Approach* (Grand Rapids: Kregel, 2004). We were contributors to this book which was awarded the Christian Book of the Year for Mission by *Christianity Today*.
16. Ross Clifford and Philip Johnson, *Jesus and the gods of the new age* (Oxford: Lion, 2001).
17. Ronald A. Hutton, *The Stations of the Sun: A History of the Ritual Year in Britain* (Oxford: Oxford University Press, 1996), 180.

CHAPTER 1: YOGA
1. Public domain image obtained from https://en.wikipedia.org/wiki/Chakra#/media/File:7_main_chackra.svg
2. Elizabeth Gilbert, *Eat, Pray, Love,* (London: Penguin, 2007), 121-122.
3. John Allan, *Yoga: A Christian Analysis* (Leicester: IVP, 1983), 62.
4. Allan, 63-64.
5. Elizabeth Shier, 'Yoga-Taboo or To Do?' *Australian Evangel*, August 1983: 23-24.
6. Christine Frost, 'Yoga and the Christian faith' available at www.iocs.cam.ac.uk/resources/texts/m_frost_yoga_and_christianity.pdf
7. 'Yoga and other such activities' in *Report of Standing Committee & Other Reports & Papers* http://socialissuesorg.au/pdf/reports/1.21.Yoga.OtherSuchActivities.Rep2015.pdf
8. John Drane, *Do Christians Know How To be Spiritual? The Rise of New Spirituality and the Mission of the Church* (London: Darton, Longman and Todd, 2005), 117-188.
9. Andrea R. Jain, 'Who Is To Say Modern Yoga Practitioners Have It All Wrong? On Hindu Origins and Yogaphobia,' *Journal of the American Academy of Religion* 82 (2014):427-471.
10. Elizabeth Gilbert, *Eat, Pray, Love,* (London: Penguin, 2007), 123.
11. On her story see Holly Vicente Robaina, 'The Truth About Yoga,' *Today's Christian Woman,* (March-April 2005): 40-43.
12. See http://caramayan.com/
13. Ross Clifford and Philip Johnson, *Jesus and the gods of the New Age* (Oxford: Lion, 2001), 171.
14. *Sydney Morning Herald* April 17, 2016 http://www.smh.com.au/national/holy-yoga-wars-spiritual-spat-as-christians-stake-claim-to-hindu-tradition-20160415-go7hia.html
15. Brooke Boon, 'A Transformed Heart – Spiritual Transformation Through Holy Yoga,' *Faith and Fitness* January 2011 available at http://faithandfitness.net/node/2893/
16. Phileena Heuertz, 'Yoga as Christian Spiritual Formation?' http://qiideas.org/articles/yoga-as-christian-spiritual-formation

NOTES

CHAPTER 2: HALLOWE'EN

1. Suzanne Sataline, 'Befriending witches is a problem in Salem, Mass.' *Pittsburgh Post-Gazette* October 31, 2006 at www.post-gazette.com/life/lifestyle/2006/10/31/Befriending-witches-is-a-problem-in-Salem-Mass
2. Phil Wyman, 'Halloween for Christians: How to Respond,' http://squarenomore.blogspot.com.au/2015/10/halloween-for-christians-how-to-respond.html
3. Wyman, 'Halloween for Christians.'
4. Father John Flader, 'Should Catholics celebrate Halloween?' *The Catholic Weekly*, October 30, 2015 see https://www.catholicweekly.com.au/should-catholics-celebrate-halloween/
5. Mark Plater, 'Children, schools and Halloween,' *British Journal of Religious Education* 35 (2013): 201-217.
6. Ronald A. Hutton, *The Stations of the Sun: A History of the Ritual Year in Britain* (Oxford: Oxford University Press, 2001), 384.
7. Ross Clifford and Philip Johnson, *The Cross Is Not Enough: Living as Witnesses to the Resurrection* (Grand Rapids: Baker, 2012).
8. See Hutton, *The Stations of the Sun*, 362.
9. Philip Johnson and John Smulo, 'Reaching Wiccan and Mother Goddess Devotees,' in *Encountering New Religious Movements: A Holistic Evangelical Approach*, eds. Irving Hexham, Stephen Rost and John W. Morehead (Grand Rapids: Kregel, 2004), 209-225.
10. For a primer on Pagan beliefs and a Christian response see Philip Johnson and Gus diZerega, *Beyond the Burning Times: A Pagan and Christian in Dialogue* (Oxford: Lion, 2007).
11. For example the conversion story of Doreen Irvine *From Witchcraft to Christ* included her claim to have been crowned England's Queen of Witches. Serious doubts about her story, covering her chronology of events and her description of rituals, were raised by the Lutheran folklore expert Bill Ellis, *Raising The Devil: Satanism, New Religions and the Media* (Lexington, Kentucky: University of Pennsylvania Press, 2000), 160-165, 190-201.
12. C. S. Lewis, *The Screwtape Letters: Letters from a senior devil to a junior devil* (Glasgow: Fount, 1977), 9.
13. See the website http://cyberhymnal.org/htm/m/i/mightyfo.htm
14. H. A. M, 'Long Live Halloween,' *Concordia Journal* 17 (1991): 374-376.
15. See the website www.haloeen.com
16. See www.scriptureunion.org.uk/3534033.id

CHAPTER 3: AROMATHERAPY

1. Naomi Coleman, 'Why you could get alternative treatment on the NHS,' *Daily Mail* available at www.dailymail.co.uk/health/article-55405/Why-alternative-treatment-NHS.html
2. Marcel Gattefossé, 'Rene-Maurice Gattefossé: The Father of Modern Aromatherapy,' *The International Journal of Aromatherapy* 4 (Winter 1992): 18-19.
3. Marguerite Maury, *Marguerite Maury's Guide to Aromatherapy: The Secret of Life and Youth: A Modern Alchemy* (Essex: C. W. Daniel, 1990), 80-81.
4. The course details appear at www.lowtonhs.wigan.sch.uk/Adult Education/AromatherapyLotionsAndPotionsAnIntroductionTo.html   <accessed 9/11/2015>

5. Gabriel Mojay, *Aromatherapy for Healing the Spirit: Restoring Emotional and Mental Balance with Essential Oils* (Rochester: Healing Arts, 1997), 46-47.
6. Kurt Schnaubelt, *Medical Aromatherapy: Healing with Essential Oils* (Berkeley: Frog, 1999), vii.
7. Scott Cunningham, *Magical Aromatherapy: The Power of Scent* (St Paul: Llewellyn, 2000), 6.
8. Aletheia Luna, '5 Aromatherapy Oils That Invoke Your Animal Spirit Guides,' http://lonerwolf.com/animal-spirit-guides
9. For example, refer to the English Christian Medical Fellowship's publication Triple Helix for information about aromatherapy, available at www.cmf.org.uk/publications
10. For further discussion and references to clinical studies see Ruth Pollard, 'Jesus Among the Alternative Healers: Sacred Oils, Aromatherapists, and the Gospel,' in *Encountering New Religious Movements: A Holistic Evangelical Approach*, ed. Irving Hexham, Stephen Rost and John W. Morehead (Grand Rapids: Kregel Academic, 2004), 265-267.
11. Michael Moseley, *Trust Me I'm A Doctor*, Series 3 episode BBC Scotland, 2015.
12. See Ross Clifford and Philip Johnson, *Jesus and the gods of the new age* (Oxford: Lion, 2001), 103.
13. David Stewart, *Healing Oils of the Bible* (Marble Hill, Missouri: CARE, 2002). Stewart's work should be read with some discernment with reference to his advice about relying exclusively on natural products to treat ailments. He is also prone to giving much credence to extra-biblical sources.

CHAPTER 4: ENERGY HEALING

1. Donna Eden with David Feinstein, *Energy Medicine: How to use your body's energies for optimum health and vitality* (London: Piatkus, 1999), 15-16.
2. Nikki Goldstein, *Lifeforce* (Sydney: Hodder, 2001), 6.
3. For the story of Usui's discovery see Paula Horan, *Empowerment through Reiki* (Wilmot: Lotus Light/Shangri-la, 1989), 21-28.
4. For further discussion see Ross Clifford and Philip Johnson, *Jesus and the gods of the new age* (Oxford: Lion, 2001), 149-169.
5. Horan, *Empowerment through Reiki*, 43-52.
6. Horan, *Empowerment through Reiki*, 17-18.
7. Bodo J. Baginski and Shalila Sharamon, *Reiki: Universal Life Energy* (Mendocino: Life Rhythm, 1988), 56-58.
8. Catherine Garrett, 'Transcendental Meditation, Reiki and Yoga: Suffering, Ritual, and Self-Transformation,' *Journal of Contemporary Religion* 16 (2001): 334.
9. See John Drane, *What is the New Age Still Saying to the Church?* (London: Marshall Pickering, 1999).
10. Linda Woodhead, 'Theology and the Fragmentation of the Self,' *International Journal of Systematic Theology* 1 (1999): 53-72.
11. Deepak Chopra, *The Future of God: A Practical Approach to Spirituality for Our Times* (New York: Crown, 2014), 19.
12. Elliot Miller, 'The Christian, Energetic Healing, New Age Paranoia,' *Christian Research Journal* 14 (Winter 1992): 24-27. Also a brief statement summarising the article is available at www.equip.org/PDF/DN068.pdf

NOTES

13. Judith White, 'Christian Reiki,' available at www.christianreiki.org/info/Articles/JudithWhiteArticle.htm
14. See www.burrswood.org.uk/our_ministry
15. See http://homeforhealth.net
16. Rob Frost, *Essence* (Eastbourne: Kingsway, 2002).
17. Ruth Pollard, 'Jesus Among the Alternative Healers,' in *Encountering New Religious Movements: A Holistic Evangelical Approach*, ed. Irving Hexham, Stephen Rost and John W. Morehead (Grand Rapids: Kregel, 2004), 269-273

CHAPTER 5: MEDITATION
1. We are using the term 'eastern' as a descriptive term only. We are critical of the way in which people popularly speak about the 'divide' between East and West.
2. Robert Booth, 'Mindfulness therapy comes at a high price for some, say experts,' *The Guardian* 26 August 2014, available at www.theguardian.com/society/2014/aug/25/mental-health-meditation
3. Melanie McDonagh, 'Mindfulness is something worse than just a smug middle-class trend,' *The Spectator*, November 2014, available at www.spectator.co.uk/2014/11/whats-wrong-with-mindfulness-more-than-you-might-think
4. Alkira Reinfrank, 'Mindfulness relaxation trial record 'overwhelming benefits' at Canberra school,' *ABC News*, 18 December 2015.
5. G. Biegel and K. W. Brown, 'Assessing the efficacy of an adapted in-class mindfulness-based training program for school-age children: A pilot study' (2011), available at http://www.mindfulschools.org/pdf/
6. 'Rupert Murdoch Is Giving Transcendental Meditation A Try,' *Huffington Post*, 23 April 2013, available at www.huffingtonpost.com/2013/04/23/rupert-murdoch-meditation-transcendental_n_3131268,html
7. Bess O'Connor, 'Teaching kids to meditate,' *Offspring Magazine* (Spring 2015): 68.
8. Maharishi Mahesh Yogi, *Transcendental Meditation* (New York: Signet, 1968), 267 & 66.
9. John Drane, 'Unknown Gods, Declining Churches, and the Spiritual Search of Contemporary Culture,' 200th Annual C.M.S. Sermon (delivered Westminster College, Cambridge, 2000). Available at http://www.cccw.cam.ac.uk/media/documents/Archive%20Seminar%20Papers%201999-2002/Unknown%20gods%20declining%20churches%20and%20the%20spiritual%20search%20of%20contemporary%20culture.pdf
10. United States District Court, District of New Jersey Civil Action No. 76-341, *Malnak v. Maharishi Mahesh Yogi* 440 F Supp. 1284 (1977).
11. William Hart, *The Art of Living: Vipassana Meditation as taught by S. N. Goenka* (San Francisco: HarperSanFrancisco, 1987).
12. Jon Kabat-Zinn, *Mindfulness Meditation for Everyday Life* (London: Judy Piatkus, 1994), 3.
13. Russell Harris, 'Embracing Your Demons: an Overview of Acceptance and Commitment Therapy,' *Psychotherapy in Australia* 12 (2006): 6.
14. Scott H. Symington and Melissa F. Symington, 'A Christian Model of Mindfulness: Using Mindfulness Principles to Support Psychological Well-Being, Value-Based Behaviour, and the Christian Spiritual Journey,' *Journal of Psychology and Christianity* 31 (2012): 71.

15. Ronald E. Purser, 'Clearing the muddled path of Traditional and Contemporary Mindfulness: A response to Monteiro, Musten, and Compson,' *Mindfulness*, 6 (2015):41.
16. Purser, 'Clearing the muddled path,' 29 & 35.
17. Daniel J. Siegel, *The Mindful Brain* (New York: Norton, 2007).
18. Robert Crosby, 'Faith and the Brain: An Interview with Dr Andrew Newberg,' *Leadership Journal* 35 (2014): 29.
19. Bill Andersen, *Walking Alongside: a theology for people-helpers* (Eugene, Oregon: Wipf & Stock, 2013), 161. Also see John Drane, *Do Christians Know How To Be Spiritual? The Rise of New Spirituality and the Mission of the Church* (London: Darton, Longman and Todd, 2005), 80-89.
20. Thich Nhat Hanh, 'Interbeing,' in *A Lifetime of Peace: Essential Writings by and about Thich Nhat Hanh*, Jennifer Schwamm Wills ed. (New York: Marlow, 2003), xv.
21. See Ross Clifford and Philip Johnson, *The Cross Is Not Enough: Living as Witnesses to the Resurrection* (Grand Rapids: Baker, 2012).
22. Symington, 'A Christian Model of Mindfulness,' 72.
23. John Calvin, *The Institutes of the Christian Religion* Vol. 1, Book 2, chapter 2, 15 & 16, trans by Ford Lewis Battles (Library of Christian Classics XX. Philadelphia: Westminster, 1960), 273-274 & 275.
24. Ambrose Ih-Ren Mong, 'Miracle of Mindfulness: Buddhist and Biblical Perspectives,' *Asia Journal of Theology* 29 (2015): 108-109.
25. David Haddon and Vail Hamilton, *TM Wants You! A Christian Response to Transcendental Meditation* (Grand Rapids: Baker, 1976), 62.
26. Start with Father George Morelli, 'Mindfulness as Known by the Church Fathers,' www.antiochan.org/mindfulness-known-church-fathers.
27. Lynda Rose, *No Other Gods* (London: Hodder, 1990), 155.
28. See http://sibc.org.au/webfiles/handout_for_meditation.doc
29. See his website www.grace-counselling.com.au
30. Tim Stead, *Mindfulness and Christian Spirituality* (London SPCK, 2016).
31. Shaun Lambert, *A Book of Sparks* (Watford: Instant Apostle, 2014).
32. See 'Walk This Way,' *Mindful* (June 2013): 66 at www.mindful.org
33. See 'Am I Hungry?' http://amihungry.com/what-is-mindful-eating/
34. Refer to www.itvmedia.co.uk/programmes/programme-planner/midwinter-spirit

CHAPTER 6: TRANSFORMATION

1. John Kehoe, *Mind Power* (Toronto: Zoetic, 1987), 23.
2. Louise Samways, *Dangerous Persuaders* (Ringwood, Victoria: Penguin, 1994), 61-95.
3. John Drane, *Do Christians Know How to be Spiritual? The Rise of New Spirituality and the Mission of the Church* (London: Darton, Longman & Todd, 2005), 55.
4. His obituary: http://www.post-gazette.com/news/obituaries/2013/02/24/Obituary-Wayne-Alderson-Made-career-helping-people-see-the-value-in-one-another/stories/201302240351 and http://triblive.com/obituaries/newsstories/3539312-74/alderson-canonsburg-hills
5. R. C. Sproul, *Stronger Than Steel: The Wayne Alderson Story* (San Francisco: Harper & Row, 1980). See the website http://www.valueoftheperson.com/

NOTES

6. R. C. Sproul, *The Hunger for Significance* (Ventura: Regal, 1991), 242-243.
7. See the teacher's manual produced for Uganda at http://www.avsi.org/wp-content/uploads/2011/09/TheValueofthePersonmanualAVSI.pdf
8. See his book *From Guru to God: An Experience of Ultimate Truth* available at http://youturnworks.com/

CHAPTER 7: ANGELS AND SPIRIT GUIDES

1. Sophy Burnham, *A Book of Angels* (New York: Ballantine, 1990), 17.
2. See 'The 'War on Christmas' in Early America' available at http://earlyamericanists.com/2013/12/23/the-early-american-war-on-christmas/#more-6614
3. Steve Saint, 'Did They Have To Die?' *Christianity Today*, 16 September 1996, 20-27.
4. See 'Hark the Herald Angel Sings' at http://nethymnal.org/htm/h/h/a/hhangels.htm
5. Paul G. Hiebert, *Anthropological Reflections on Missiological Issues* (Grand Rapids: Baker, 1994), 189-201.
6. Ross Clifford and Philip Johnson, *Riding the Rollercoaster: How the Risen Christ Empowers Life* (Sydney: Strand, 1998), 74-75.
7. For a sample sermon see Ross Clifford, *Apologetic Preaching and Teaching for the Church and the Marketplace* (Macquarie Park: Morling, 2011), 100-104.

CHAPTER 8: ASTROLOGY, TAROT NUMEROLOGY

1. John Drane, Ross Clifford, and Philip Johnson, *Beyond Prediction: The Tarot and Your Spirituality* (Oxford: Lion, 2001).
2. Dave Tomlinson, *The Post Evangelical* (London: Triangle/SPCK, 1995), 143.
3. For more discussion see Philip Johnson, Simeon Payne and Peter Wilson, 'Toward a Contextualized Astrological Apologetic, with a Case Study for Booth Ministry Outreach,' *Missiology* 36 (2008): 185-200.
4. John Drane, *Do Christians Know How To Be Spiritual? The Rise of New Spirituality and the Mission of the Church* (London: Darton, Longman and Todd, 2005), 118.
5. Joseph Campbell and Richard Roberts, *Tarot Revelations* (San Anselmo, California: Vernal Equinox, 1987), 253-254.
6. Drane, *Do Christians Know How To Be Spiritual?*, 117.
7. For more discussion see Ross Clifford and Philip Johnson, *Jesus and the gods of the new age* (Oxford: Lion, 2001).
8. See http://www.sanctus1.co.uk/ and Ben Edson, 'An Exploration into the Missiology of the Emerging Church in the UK Through the Narrative of Sanctus1,' *International Journal for the Study of the Christian Church* 6 (2006): 24-37.
9. Ross Clifford, *John Warwick Montgomery's Legal Apologetic: An Apologetic for all Seasons* (Bonn: Verlag für Kultur und Wissenschaft, 2004; Eugene, Oregon: Wipf and Stock, forthcoming 2016), 227.

CHAPTER 9: CHRISTIAN BLESSINGS

1. Based on Philip's forthcoming book *The Noah Challenge: Resurrecting Our Conscience for God's Creatures.*
2. 'Animals', *The Vicar of Dibley*, season 1, episode 6, originally broadcast in

1994, and rebroadcasted in series reruns worldwide.

3. Caitlin Marsh, 'Church hosts Vicar of Dibley-style carol service for animals,' *Daily Echo*, 22 December 2014, available at www.bournemouthecho.co.uk/news/11681045.

4. 'Auckland's pets blessed in church,' 5 October 2015 at www.stuff.co.nz/auckland/72679738/Aucklands-pets-blessed-in-church

5. Patricia Appelbaum, *St Francis of America: How a Thirteenth-Century Friar Became America's Most Popular Saint* (Chapel Hill: University of North Carolina Press, 2015), 149.

6. Video of the 2013 service is accessed at www.youtube.com/watch?v=rdd7sCFCkkA. Also refer to www.stjohnthedivine.org/visit/calendar/events/liturgy-worship/12115/feast-of-saint-francis-and-blessing-of-the-animals

7. See www.edola.org/st-francis-blessing-of-the-animals/

8. 'Blessing of the animals,' www.elca.org/en/Living-Lutheran/Stories/2013/03/130301c and www.gracelutherannc.com/wp/blessing-of-the-animals-service-oct-6th/

9. See www.umcdiscipleship.org/resources/a-service-for-the-blessing-of-animals

10. Jeff Brumley, 'Baptists embrace pet blessings,' *Baptist News* 12 October, 2012, https://baptistnews.com/ministry/congregations/item/7905-pet-blessings-becoming-baptist-practice

11. See www.cccdt.org/centraldogpark.html

12. Colin Brown, 'Animals in the NT,' in *The New International Dictionary of New Testament Theology*, Vol. 1 Rev. Ed., ed. Colin Brown (Exeter: Paternoster, 1980), 116.

13. Scott Bader-Saye, 'Imaging God Through Peace with Animals: An Election for Blessing,' *Studies in Christian Ethics* 14 (2001): 1-13.

14. David Instone-Brewer, *Traditions of the Rabbis from the Era of the New Testament, Vol 1 Prayer and Agriculture* (Grand Rapids; Cambridge: Eerdmans, 2004).

15. William Dumbrell, *Covenant and Creation: An Old Testament Covenantal Theology* (Homebush West: Lancer; Exeter: Paternoster, 1984).

16. Martin Luther, *Lectures on Genesis Chapters 6-14*, in *Luther's Works*, Vol 2 ed. Jaroslav Pelikan (St Louis: Concordia 1960), 144.

17. Richard Bauckham, *Bible and Ecology: Rediscovering the Community of Creation* (London: Darton, Longman and Todd, 2010).

18. *Midrash Tanhuma Yelammedenu*, Noah 3, translated by Samuel A. Berman (Hoboken, New Jersey: KTAV Publishing, 1996), 50.

19. Ruth Padilla DeBorst, 'God's Earth and God's People: Relationships Restored,' *Journal of Latin American Theology* 5 (2010): 6-17.

20. J. Richard Middleton, *A New Heaven and a New Earth: Reclaiming Biblical Eschatology* (Grand Rapids: Baker Academic, 2014).

21. John G. Gibbs, *Creation and Redemption: A Study in Pauline Theology* (Leiden: Brill, 1971).

22. Colin G. Kruse, *Paul's Letter to the Romans* (Grand Rapids; Cambridge: Eerdmans, 2012), 342.

23. Ryan Patrick McLaughlin, 'Evidencing the Eschaton: Progressive-Transformative Animal Welfare in the Church Fathers,' *Modern Theology* 27 (2011): 121-146.

NOTES

24. Rocco Bogognoni, 'No Animals in the New Paradise? The 'Hall of Philia' in Antioch and the Patristic Exegesis of Isaiah's 'Peaceable Kingdom', *Studia Patristica* 44 (2010): 21-26.

25. William J. Short, 'Restoring Eden: Medieval Legends of Saints and Animals,' *Continuum* 2 (1992): 43-57.

26. Alastair Minnis, *From Eden to Eternity: Creations of Paradise in the Later Middle Ages* (Philadelphia: University of Pennsylvania Press, 2015).

27. Philip C. Almond, *Adam and Eve in Seventeenth Century Thought* (Cambridge: Cambridge University Press, 1995).

28. J. Richard Middleton, *The Liberating Image: The Imago Dei in Genesis 1* (Grand Rapids: Brazos, 2005). Richard Bauckham, *Living With Other Creatures: Green Exegesis and Theology* (Waco: Baylor University Press, 2011), 14-62.

29. John Calvin, *Commentary on the Epistle to the Romans*, trans. by Francis Sibson (London: L. B. Seeley and Sons, 1834), 331. See book 3, chapter 9, 5 in *Institutes of the Christian Religion*, Vol 1, trans. Ford Lewis Battles (Philadelphia: Westminster, 1960), 717.

30. Alastair Minnis, 'The Restoration of All Things: John Bradford's Refutation of Aquinas on Animal Resurrection,' *Journal of Medieval and Early Modern Studies* 45 (2015): 323-342.

31. Bishop Joseph Butler, 'Of A Future Life' in *The Analogy of Religion Natural and Revealed* (London: George Bell, [1736] 1902), 81-98. Richard Dean, *An Essay on the Future Life of Brutes, introduced with observations upon evil*, 2 Vols. (Manchester, 1767).

32. *The Works of John Wesley* (Vol 6; New York: Harper, 1826), 252-261.

33. 'On Cruelty to the Brute Creation,' in *The Works of Augustus Toplady* (London: Chidley, 1837 [1794]), 443-446.

34. Gregory Bassham, 'Some Dogs Go To Heaven: Lewis on Animal Salvation,' in *The Chronicles of Narnia and Philosophy: The Lion, The Witch, and the Worldview*, eds. Gregory Bassham and Jerry L. Walls (Chicago; LaSalle: Open Court, 2005), 273-285.

35. Robert Milburn, *Early Christian Art and Architecture*, (Berkeley; Los Angeles: University of California Press, 1988).

36. The mosaic is in the Misis Mosaic Museum, Turkey see www.39fss.com/docs/odr/Misis.pdf

37. Adreina Contessa, 'Noah's Ark and the Ark of the Covenant in Spanish and Sephardic Medieval Manuscripts,' in *Between Judaism and Christianity: Art Historical Essays in Honor of Elisheva (Elisabeth) Revel-Neher*, ed. Katrin Kogman-Appel and Mati Meyer (Leiden: Brill, 2009), 175.

38. Paul E. Kretzmann, *Christian Art in the Place and in the Form of Lutheran Worship* (St Louis, Missouri: Concordia Publishing House, 1921), 29.

39. Dom Ambrose Agius, *God's Animals* (London: Catholic Study Circle for Animal Welfare, 1970), 105.

40. 'Animals at Church,' *Examiner* [Launceston, Tasmania] 17 May 1907, 8. Adam Justice, 'Peru: Lima church hosts animal St Francis Day blessing of animals,' at www.ibtimes.co.uk/peru-lima-church-hosts-animal-st-francis-day-blessing-of-animals-1522511

41. Kenneth Stevenson, 'Animal Rites: The Four Living Creatures in Patristic Exegesis and Liturgy,' in *Studia Patristica* 34, ed. Maurice F. Wiles and Edward J. Yarnold (Leuven: Peeters, 2001), 488-489.

TABOO OR TO DO?

42. E. A. Wallis Budge Ed., *The Ethiopian Synaxarium* (Cambridge UK: Cambridge University Press, 1928), 222.
43. Kathryn Shevelow, *For the Love of Animals: The Rise of the Animal Protection Movement* (New York: Henry Holt, 2008).
44. Keith A. Francis, 'Sermons: Themes and Developments' in *The Oxford Handbook of the British Sermon 1689-1901*, Keith A. Francis and William Gibson Eds. (Oxford: Oxford University Press, 2012), 37.
45. *The Duty of Humanity to Inferior Creatures, Deduced from Reason and Scripture (Abridged from Dr Primatt)*, ed. Arthur Broome (London, 1831), note on 129-130.
46. Arthur Penrhyn Stanley, *The Creation of Man: A Sermon preached at Whitehall Chapel July 9, 1865* (Oxford and London: Parker, 1865). Arthur W. Moss, *Valiant Crusade: The History of the R. S. P.C.A.* (London: Cassell, 1961), 205.
47. For example, 'Kindness to Animals,' *Sydney Morning Herald* 30 May 1890, 3; 'United Church Service' *Morwell Advertiser* [Victoria] 8 November 1907, 3;
48. 'Tasmanian SPCA. The Annual Meeting,' *Mercury*, 17 March 1909, 6.
49. *Christchurch Presbytery* Vol LXII, 9 August 1905, 4. 'Prevention of Cruelty,' *Press*, 7 February 1906, 8. 'Clergy and the S.P.C.A.,' *Colonist* 27 June 1908, 4.
50. 'Animal Sunday,' *Wanganui Chronicle*, [NZ] 29 October 1908, 8.
51. *Taranaki Daily News* 'An Appeal For the Animals' and 'The Animal Creation' 27 October 1914 and 7 October 1916.
52. 'Our Humble Subjects,' *The Adelaide Advertiser*, 13 October 1945, 8.
53. Elsie K. Morton, 'Man and the Animals: 'Welfare Week' Appeal,' *New Zealand Herald* 24 October 1925, 1.
54. See www.worldanimalday.org.uk/ An early call to celebrate is Elsie K. Morton, 'Our Friends the Animals: World Day Observance,' *New Zealand Herald* 3 October 1936, 8.
55. Roger D. Sorrell, *St Francis of Assisi and Nature: Tradition and Innovation in Western Christian Attitudes toward the Environment* (New York; Oxford: Oxford University Press, 1988).
56. See 'Safari Tourism – Paying to Kill,' ABC-TV Four Corners broadcast March 16, 2016 see http://www.abc.net.au/4corners/stories/2016/03/14/4422650.htm
57. http://www.cbc.ca/radio/thecurrent/up-to-a-billion-birds-die-flying-into-windows-in-north-america-each-year-better-design-could-change-that-1.2907446
58. Michael S. Northcott, 'BP, the Blowout and the Bible Belt: Why Conservative Christianity Does Not Conserve Creation,' *Expository Times* 122 (2010): 117-126.
59. The term speciesist was coined by Peter Singer but popularised by Richard D. Ryder, *Animal Revolution: Changing Attitudes toward Speciesism* (Oxford: Basil Blackwell, 1989).
60. Rod Preece, *Brute Souls, Happy Beasts and Evolution: The Historical Status of Animals* (Toronto: UBC Press, 2005), 7.
61. Tony Sargent, *Animal Rights and Wrongs: A Biblical Perspective* (London: Hodder & Stoughton, 1996).
62. Philip Sampson, 'The Curious Case of the Kind Evangelicals,' *Ethics in Brief* 20 (Spring 2015) available at www.klice.co.uk/uploads/Ethics%20in%Brief/EiB_Sampson_20_3_WEB.pdf

63. J. Y. Jones, *Worship Not The Creature: Animal Rights and the Bible* (Ventura: Nordskog Publishing, 2009), 115-160.

64. Norm Phelps, *The Longest Struggle: Animal Advocacy from Pythagoras to PETA* (New York: Lantern, 2007).

65. Eugene C. Hargrove Ed. *The Animal Rights/Environmental Ethics Debate: The Environmental Perspective* (Albany: State University of New York Press, 1992).

66. Andrew Linzey, *Christianity and the Rights of Animals* (New York: Crossroad, 1989).

67. Lisa Kemmerer and Anthony J. Nocella II Eds. *Call to Compassion: Religious Perspectives on Animal Advocacy* (New York: Lantern, 2011).

68. Robin Jean Brown, *How to ROAR: Pet Loss Grief Recovery* (Athens, Georgia: Spring Water Publishing, 2005).

69. Millie Cordaro, 'Pet Loss and Disenfranchised Grief: Implications for Mental Health Counseling,' *Journal of Mental Health Counseling* 34 (2012): 283-294.

70. Kenneth Brown, 'Pastoral concern related to the psychological stress caused by the death of a companion animal,' *Mental Health, Religion and Culture* 9 (2006): 411-422.

71. Barney Zwartz, 'Creature Comforts,' *The Age* 21 August 2006 available at http://www.theage.com.au/news/in-depth/creature-comfort/2006/08/21/1156012473730.html.

72. Michael S. Koppel, 'Companions in Presence: Animal Assistants and Eldercare,' *Pastoral Psychology* 60 (2011): 108.

73. Jerilyn E. Felton, 'Ministry with Dogs: Where Spiritual and Pastoral Care Have a Wet Nose and Four Feet,' *Human Development* 33/4 (Winter 2012): 48.

74. http://www.newskete.org/our-dogs.html

75. See 'A service for animal welfare' at www.rspca.org.uk/ and Andrew Linzey, *Animal Rites: Liturgies of Animal Care* (London: SCM, 1999).

76. Matt Bamford, 'Hundreds flock to church for Sydney pet blessing,' *North Shore Times*, 3 September 2013 available at www.dailytelegraph.com.au/newslocal/north-shore/hundreds-flock-to-church-for-Sydney-pet-blessings/story-fngr8h9d-1226709608011

77. *St George and Sutherland Shire Leader*, October 6, 2015, 18 available at www.theleader.com.au/story/3401968/bless-your-pets-and-remember-st-francis-of-assisi

78. See the Church's website www.saintjohnorthodox.org/pets-animals-blessed/

CHAPTER 10: MARTIAL ARTS

1. Arthur Conan Doyle, 'The Empty House' in *The Complete Original Illustrated Sherlock Holmes* (Secaucus, New Jersey: Castle Books, 1978), 453.

2. Emelyne Godfrey, 'Sherlock Holmes and the Mystery of Baritsu,' *History Today* (May 2009): 4-5.

3. *The Samurai* consisted of 128 episodes and was broadcast from 1962-65. *Phantom Agents* comprised 130 episodes and was broadcast from 1964-1966. *The Green Hornet* only comprised one season of 26 episodes that were broadcast in 1966-1967.

4. Peter Lewis, *Martial Arts* (London: Bison, 1987), 124-125.

5. Christmas Humphreys, *Zen Buddhism*, (London: Unwin, 1957), 230.

6. 'Enter The Dragon' Special Edition, Warner Bros Home Video, 2001.

7. See Meir Shahar, *The Shaolin Monastery: History, Religion, and the Chinese Martial Arts* (Honolulu: University of Hawaii Press, 2008).

8. Bob Larson, *Larson's Book of Cults* (Wheaton: Tyndale House, 1982), 293-301.

9. Einat Bar-On Cohen, 'Opening and Closing Ritual in Aikido and Karate and the Dismantling of Violence,' *Journal of Ritual Studies* 23 (2009): 29-44.

10. B. J. Oropeza, 'Should A Christian Practice The Martial Arts?' available at www.equip.org/article/should-a-christian-practice-the-martial-arts/ . Also the two-part article Erwin de Castro, B.J. Oropeza and Ron Rhodes, 'Enter the Dragon?' *Christian Research Journal* (Fall 1993) and (Winter 1994).

11. Pat Means, *The Mystical Maze* (San Bernardino: Campus Crusade for Christ, 1976), 123.

12. Andrea Molle, 'Towards a Sociology of *budō*: Studying the Implicit Religious Issues,' *Implicit Religion* 13 (2010): 86.

13. Molle, 'Towards a Sociology of *budō*,' 90-91.

14. 'Calling All Angels,' *Trust* (Autumn 2016): 5.

15. Rob Boddice, 'Manliness and 'The Morality of Field Sports': E. A. Freeman and Anthony Trollope, 1869-71,' *Historian* 70 (2008): 1-29.

16. See http://www.mmafighting.com/2016/4/12/11413100/mma-fighter-joao-carvalho-dies-following-tko-loss-in-ireland

17. 'Mixed Martial Arts and Christianity: 'Where Feet, Fist and Faith Collide," *The Conversation*, January 5, 2015 available at http://theconversation.com/mixed-martial-arts-and-christianity-where-feet-fist-and-faith-collide-34836

18. Diana Looser, 'The 'Risk Society' and Martial Arts Training in New Zealand,' *Journal of Asian Martial Arts* 15 (2006): 9-23.

19. Stephen Donaldson, *Lord's Foul Bane* 'The Chronicles of Thomas Covenant, The Unbeliever' (Glasgow: Fontana, 1978), 262.

20. Ross Clifford and Philip Johnson, *The Cross Is Not Enough: Living as Witnesses to the Resurrection* (Grand Rapids: Baker, 2012).

21. See his website www.fatherdave.org

22. See http://www.stmartinswalsall.co.uk/activities/community-groups/

CONTINUING THE CONVERSATION

1. Bede, *Ecclesiastical History of the English People*, trans. Leo Shirley-Price (London: Penguin, 1990), 91-92.

2. John Drane, *The McDonaldization of the Church* (London: Darton, Longman & Todd, 2000), 176-178.

3. N. T. Wright, *Acts for Everyone: Part 2 Chapters 13-28* (London: SPCK; Louisville: Westminster John Knox, 2008), 93.

4. Paulo Coelho, *The Pilgrimage* (New York: HarperCollins, 1999), 22.